Child's Work:

Taking Children's Choices Seriously

Child's Work:

Taking Children's Choices Seriously

by Nancy Wallace

Holt Associates
Cambridge, Mass.

Grateful acknowledgment is made to Alfred A. Knopf, Inc., for permission to reprint the poem "Exclusive," from *The Dead and The Living* by Sharon Olds, copyright © 1983 by Sharon Olds.

Portions of Chapter 7 appeared earlier in *Mothering,* Volume #38, page 83, and are used here with permission.

The publishers wish to thank volunteer typists Maggi Elliott and Sue Smith.

Cover design by Dave Sullivan
Illustrations by Vita Wallace

ISBN 0-913677-06-X
Library of Congress Catalog Card Number: 90-82389

Acknowledgments

A writer always needs first readers. I especially want to thank my mother, Benji and Helen Brown, and Merloyd Lawrence for filling that role without complaint and for giving so freely of their critical advice and encouragement.

To my publisher, Pat Farenga, my heartfelt thanks for his unquestioning belief in this project and for his determination to bring it to life, and to my friend and editor, Susannah Sheffer, special thanks for being there from the start and in every way since.

Finally, thank you Ishmael and Vita, as always my main characters.

Contents

Foreword
by Susannah Sheffer

Nancy Wallace's second book says so many things that need to be said. Since her first book, *Better Than School,* was published in 1983, Nancy has been one of the home education movement's foremost writers, over and over again inspiring parents to feel comfortable helping their children learn outside of school. Now, with *Child's Work,* Nancy shows us in even more depth and detail what happens when children are able to choose their activities and direct their own educations. The book lets us see how Vita and Ishmael, the young children of *Better Than School,* have grown and become increasingly skilled at their chosen work. It also explores the ways in which all children learn and the conditions under which they are most likely to flourish.

So many books about education talk about what adults can do to or for children. How should we teach? What should we teach? When should we begin teaching? These are the questions that concern most educational writers. *Child's Work* is one of a very few books that look at what *children* do, what *children* know, how *they* go about making sense of the world.

Nancy Wallace's special skill, a skill that informs every page of *Child's Work,* is her ability to look at children doing even the most ordinary things and recognize them as builders of their own knowledge and understanding. She sees that in reciting passages of *Winnie-the-Pooh* over and over again, the young Vita and Ishmael were actually internalizing the patterns of written language in ways that would affect their own development as writers later on. She theorizes that Ishmael's early fascination with block building had a direct connection to his later work as a composer and musician. *Child's Work* is about these connections, about the anatomy of children's learning rather than simply its product.

Though *Child's Work* is clearly about how well children learn on their own, it also demonstrates that "on their own" does not mean "without the involvement of anyone else." The book looks at how children use the adults around them as they go about their learning, and it suggests ways in which adults can be most helpful to children. We hear how Nancy learned to value what her children did and to respond in ways that would help rather than discourage them.

Vita and Ishmael are impressively competent at their chosen work, so much so that some readers may think this is a story about prodigies and consider it irrelevant to their own children or children they know. *Child's Work* is, indeed, about Vita's and Ishmael's skill at music, composition, art, and writing. Yet if this were all that Nancy had to tell, the book would not be as useful as it in fact is. For Nancy, the most interesting question about Vita and Ishmael is not, "What can they do?" but "Why have they been able to do so much; what conditions have allowed them to flourish?" If we think of Vita and Ishmael as prodigies, we avoid having to think about what helped them become as competent as they are. What if all children had the time to experiment, to pursue their own work, to draw on the resources around them? Might we then discover that children's capacities, and their ability to find work they love and pursue it wholeheartedly, are greater than we ever dreamed?

If Vita and Ishmael are in fact different from many other children, I suspect this is because all through their lives, their activities have been treated with the respect granted to any serious work. Nancy tells us that at first she interrupted the children's doll play without giving much thought to how much this upset them. Gradually, she learned that they felt just as frustrated by those interruptions as Nancy felt when someone interrupted her while she was writing. In other words, Vita and Ishmael saw themselves as busy, as engaged in important work. Much of *Child's Work* is the story of how Nancy came to see this as well, and to treat her children accordingly. Thus, her story is not about learning how to make superchildren — how to turn her children into something out of the ordinary. Rather, it is about learning to recognize that the ordinary activities of childhood are as valuable and as deserving of respect as any important adult work.

Some friends of mine used to use the word "work" to describe the ordinary things that their eighteen-month-old son did around the house. If he was banging pots together and fitting the smaller ones inside the larger ones, as eighteen-month-olds often do, they would say, "He's doing his pot work." I used to laugh, but I learned something from these friends. I believe they used that language to remind themselves that what their son was doing was important. It helped them remember that if they had to disturb him — to move him out of the way so that they could cook dinner, for example — they should do it with the same courtesy that they would use if they were forced to interrupt another adult at work.

It's easy to imagine the effect that this parental response must have had on the boy's own view of himself and his activities. Similarly, I suspect that Nancy's recognition of the value of her children's activities is, more than anything else, what has allowed Vita and Ishmael to flourish. The goal of *Child's Work*, it seems to me, is to encourage all of us to give our children's activities the same recognition.

In publishing *Child's Work*, we at Holt Associates are continuing a twenty-year-long tradition of supporting children's self-directed learning and those who write about it. By keeping the books of author/educator John Holt in print, by publishing *Growing Without Schooling* magazine, and now by publishing *Child's Work*, we hope to demonstrate that what children do as they make their way into the world is more often than not meaningful, sensible, and truly educational.

INTRODUCTION

All in a Day's Work

Katie is desperate to be an adult, and this is what I find most interesting about her. At the table, when we drink from glasses, she wants to drink from a glass too. Lorrie cut her a slice of apple which she began to eat. Then Lorrie started eating an entire apple, the way adults do, eating bit by bit around the core. So Katie had to eat that way, too, even though it took twenty minutes.

— My father, Hubert Marshall, writing about his granddaughter and my niece, Katie Marshall

When I was a teenager I often skipped school to spend the afternoon people-watching at the San Francisco zoo. These were the days of outrage. We thrived on outrage like nothing else. We were outraged by our parents' protectiveness and concern; we were outraged by the cops who harassed us, looking for stashes of marijuana; we were outraged by the Vietnam war and the government violence against Black Power activists like Huey Newton and Bobby Seale; we were outraged by businessmen in suits and by ticky-tacky houses and by the drivers of big American cars.

My own particular outrage was directed at the parents who brought their young children to the zoo. I was outraged by their lack of sensitivity to their children's magnified sense of time. The parents trotted along from animal cage to animal cage, dragging their children with them, unaware that to their children each moment encompassed a year of discoveries. These parents looked only at the caged animals, laughed only at what everyone expected them to think was funny, and expected their children to laugh too. Their children, meanwhile, living so much closer to the ground because of their size, wriggled their hands free from their parents' grasp whenever they could, and lingered — not over the caged animals, but over the bits of candy wrapper that their parents blindly stepped on, the chipped and peeling paint on the low green railings in front of the animal cages, and the trampled pieces of hotdog bun and popcorn that littered the zoo pathways. They were fascinated less by the caged exotic birds than by the sparrows and pigeons pecking at the zoo litter.

The children I watched ran when they weren't supposed to run, chased after the birds when they were supposed to be staring into cages or eating picnic lunches, lingered here and skipped ahead there. They moved along within no discernable time-frame, guided only by their curiosity and hunger for discovery.

In the revised edition of *How Children Learn*, the late educational critic John Holt writes, "If we give children access to enough of the world, including our own lives and work in that world, they will see clearly enough what things are truly important to us and to others, and they will make for themselves a better path into that world than we could make for them."

Perhaps John's use of the word "give" in his opening phrase would be better changed to "allow," to make the sentence begin, "If we *allow* children," but in any case, "access" is the important word, the important concept. Aaron Falbel, in his thesis about the Danish free school, *Friskolen 70*, says that "access implies making someone an offer — an offer that they can refuse. Exposure on the other hand means subjecting someone to an experience.... Exposure is something done to you; access refers to proximity, availability."

The parents I watched at the zoo brought their children there, not because it was important to their own lives and work, but because they thought it was important, as good parents, to expose their children to wild, albeit caged, animals. They would never have believed it if someone had told them that, despite their yanks and grabs and growing impatience with their children's pace, what was so valuable about their outing was that they were allowing their children access to litter and the infinite patterns made by peeling paint on metal railings.

Meanwhile, what I noticed with a kind of awe and envy was that even at the tender ages of two or three, the children seldom complained as their parents attempted to pull them along and show them the sights. Automatically, it seemed, they just kept wriggling their little hands free. When they did make a peep, they accepted, happily, the cotton candy and popsicles offered them as pacifiers, and then went back to their work, as if they knew no other way.

Although I never would have used the word "work," then, to describe what these children did at the zoo, I use it now because it is the best way I know to describe the process that children go through as they attempt to make their own pathways into the world. It is fashionable, and I think correct, to say that children learn more in their first five years than they do in the rest of their lives put together. Yet generally, we call what children do *work* only later, after they start school. Schoolwork — work that adults assign to children — is the only serious child's work that, as a society, we acknowledge.

Yet at the zoo, I was watching determined young scientists and explorers, quietly and patiently battling the adults they most loved and admired in order to better understand the environment they were growing up in. And what was this activity, really? Child's play? Hardly. Part of the fascination for me then — the outrage — was knowing that eventually these children would tire of their battle. They would grow taller and learn to stare into the animal cages the way they were supposed to. The thought that they would learn to laugh at what was expected, at the expense of going blind to the peeling paint and the trampled popcorn, horrified me. Already I realized the value, the beauty, the importance of child's work, and the tragedy of its loss. Yet, as I have said, I didn't then equate the exuberant quality of children, their eye for detail, and their amazing sense of time, with work.

In fact, although I was then beginning to do the work that would occupy me for the next twenty years — that of watching young children — I was sure I was playing, too. How else could I describe my escape from schoolwork? Sitting there at the zoo, I would have been able to tell you only that I was determined to escape the work I knew I ought to be doing so that I could spend my time doing what I loved. It took me years and years to realize that even then, I had begun on a life's work, and that it was legitimate to equate what I loved doing with work. It was my own two children, Ishmael and Vita, who first taught me this, and other children since have, by example, drummed the idea into my head when I have wavered.

My children's insistence on pursuing their own work, and all that I have learned from them about how children learn as they go about their work, is what interests me here. In my first book, *Better Than School,* I told the story of how my husband Bob and I took Ishmael out of school and taught him, and later Vita, at home. From our first battle to win legal permission to take Ishmael out of school, to the ways we negotiated our educational program with the local school authorities, to the ways we learned to organize our own lives and work — Bob's as a translator and mine as a writer — around our children's needs, *Better Than School* provides a concrete picture of how home-schooling worked for one family. Many of our experiences, joys, sorrows, frustrations, and unexpected pleasures were ones that only we Wallaces could have shared; others were more universal. Yet by describing the ways we found to provide our children with the tools, teachers, and environments they needed, I hoped to offer other parents an example of how families that are determined enough, inventive enough, and insistent enough can find solutions to seemingly insurmountable problems.

Child's Work takes my story one step further, by looking at *how* Vita and Ishmael, now twelve and fifteen, have drawn on the materials and people in their environment to explore, define, and finally build their own paths into the world. In doing so, *Child's Work* moves beyond homeschooling — beyond a discussion of parents' roles as teachers, protectors, and negotiators for their children — to a look at children's work itself, at the choices children make about their own learning.

We began homeschooling when Ishmael was eight years old. After a long year and a half of agony and struggle, he had finally managed to make clear to us that he *needed* to read and write and do the other work that was important to him, and that the school regime, with its "papers" and busy work, its timed tests, and most of all, its insistence that children learn specific skills in a specific and non-negotiable sequence, made his work impossible. At the time, taking Ishmael out of school seemed to us like an act of desperation. He was falling apart and we felt we had no other alternative.

Although from the start we were anxious to help Ishmael heal from the damage that school had done him, and excited by the possibilities of teaching him ourselves, we had very little idea of what those possibilities were. In 1979, when we began, there were fewer than ten thousand homeschoolers scattered across the country. We had had almost no contact with experienced homeschoolers, and John Holt's newsletter *Growing Without Schooling* was just in its fledgling stages. We hadn't yet found anybody who could, out of his or her own experience, answer questions like, "What happens when children learn in a truly non-competitive environment?" "What happens when children are never told to memorize their multiplication tables, and in fact don't even know that memorizing math facts is something that children are routinely expected to do?" "What happens to children who have never been taught to doubt their own competence to learn?"

My friend Susannah Sheffer, the current editor of *Growing Without Schooling*, wrote in issue #59, "If we only observe children in school, we can't tell whether children would learn to read if they weren't forced into it or rewarded for it. We can't tell at what age they would naturally take an interest in the activity. Only when we look at children who are allowed to determine when and how they will learn (as most children in school, of course, are not), can we begin to understand the range of what is 'normal.'"

When we first took Ishmael out of school nobody had yet had enough experience to tell us what was "normal," what was possible. In the beginning, at least, we had to discover it all for ourselves. Eventually, what came to seem to us the most normal was, in fact, our biggest discovery, and one that in many ways led to all the possibilities that homeschooling has since opened up for us. It was this: that when Vita and Ishmael are busy, they are simply busy. Despite the ways and attitudes of the rest of the world, they refuse to see a distinction between schoolwork and everything else they do. They are genuinely baffled when people ask, "But what do you do just for fun?" as if to imply that doing anything of real value and importance couldn't by definition be classified as giving light-hearted pleasure, and that after a hard day's work we all need a change. "But why?" I see Vita and Ishmael wonder.

Once, when a reporter came to interview Ishmael, he was so amazed by Ishmael's bemused attitude that he said, "Oh, come on now, isn't there anything you have to do that you don't like?"

Ishmael thought and thought, his chin resting in the cup of his hand. Finally, to save time, and almost certainly because I was feeling desperate to appear at least somewhat conventional, I said, "Well, you don't really like math that much, do you, Ishmael?"

"Yes, I do," he said. "Algebra is really beautiful — at least when it works."

"What about taking out the trash, then," the reporter persisted.

"Well, " Ishmael said thoughtfully, "I haven't done much of that. I'll have to try it."

For Vita and Ishmael, there is no such thing as child's play. The joy, the uncontainable giggles, the lingering here and skipping ahead there — it's all in a day's work for them. That is what this book is all about.

Seeing Our Children

When you are watching a bird and are looking at the feathers, the colours, the beak, the size and the lovely shape of the bird, then you are giving your heart, your mind and body, everything that you have to watch it. And then you are really part of that bird.

— From *On Education*, by Krishnamurti

"**R**eading about Ishmael and Vita," John Holt wrote in his introduction to *Better Than School,* "we can only be struck by how very personal, idiosyncratic, and unique are their ways of learning. It is tempting to think that most children have rather more orthodox ways of exploring and making sense of the world. But it is not so; all children move into the world in personal and idiosyncratic ways, and no two do it alike."

Unfortunately schools, with their curriculums based on the assumption that most children learn in given sequences and within certain time frames that can be considered normal, often blur John's very important observation for us. My mother said to me recently, after a hard game of ping-pong with the kids, "Too many parents never see their children."

"Yes, I know, " I said. "Between school, day care, their work, and their kids' social lives it's pretty hard." I just assumed that what struck her about us was how much time we spend together. But I was wrong.

"What I mean," she explained, "is that it's so hard for parents to *really* see their children." She was right, of course. Too often, when we look for our children, they are hidden from us by our own fears about how well they are measuring up to the schools' expectations and by our equally troubled worries about the harmful influences of peers. Where *are* our children? Who are they? I am fortunate. Because my children are not in school, these sorts of worries don't stand in my way. Yet even for me, there is no harder job than trying to see my children. Still, it is the most interesting and satisfying job I know.

Vita and Ishmael are remarkably close, and sometimes it seems as if they do everything together. When, in the middle of one of her little blue journal notebooks, Vita decided that it was time to give her readers her vital statistics, her major vital statistic seemed to be Ishmael.

> I am ten years old, but I am soon going to be eleven. I play the violin and the piano... I also sing in The Children's Chorus and write songs for it. I do not go to school and neither does my brother, Ishmael, who is fourteen. My parents are Bob and Nancy and my name is Vita (Vita

means "life.") I live on Irving Place and we call our house "The Irving Place Conservatory." My brother has written three operettas and one short opera which have all been performed at The First Street Playhouse, C. Fellman directing. I think that's all I need to say.

If Vita's life is totally wrapped up in Ishmael's, though, his is equally wrapped up in hers. Vita and Ishmael take it for granted that they share most of the same interests, and they eagerly pursue them together. They play four-hand piano music together, sharing the same bench. They improvise big stormy pieces, or write music and critique each other's "student" pieces when The Irving Place Conservatory is in session. They can't imagine what long walks or car rides would be like without endless chatter about books, or serious discussions about the monumental symphonies they plan to write someday. They can't imagine not both loving to roller-skate, going to the opera, or *Pickwick Papers*.

Visiting friends often see Ishmael and Vita holding hands as they roller-skate down the street, Vita adjusting Ishmael's tie before a family concert, or Ishmael's face lighting up with delight when Vita manages to sing a multiphonic — a deep throaty note with an audible harmonic sounding above it. Our friends say, "What an amazing relationship those two have." "Yes," I agree. And yet it is their almost black and white differences that seem most amazing to me, and make the job of really seeing them, as my mother put it, all the harder.

In the morning when I go to wake Vita and Ishmael up, if Vita isn't already awake, lying on her stomach in bed and reading one of her old favorites, usually *Little Women*, I see her eyes open instantly, and from her first glance they sparkle with energy. Ishmael, on the other hand, makes waking up look like total agony. His eyelids are *so* heavy. His body is like a lump of clay waiting to be shaped. Even when he finally gets dressed (okay, no shoes yet, his thick hair flying in all directions) and is sitting at the table with oatmeal steam drifting into his face, his eyes close and his head suddenly droops. Poor Ishmael. Will he ever wake up and butter his toast or decide if he wants raisins or bananas on his mush?

Perhaps because the art of waking up in the morning isn't part of the school curriculum, we are all aware of just how we wake up, and amused by our idiosyncratic waking habits. We talk about late-night people and early-morning people; people who can't eat a thing for breakfast and others who can wolf down whole stacks of pancakes. "I can't do anything until I've had my first cup of coffee," a friend says, and we smile, taking it for granted that she knows her morning responses that well.

I like to think that as I do with their early morning rising, I can simply stand back, in wonder and amazement, and see my children's idiosyncratic approaches to the world, and yet all too often, I am surprised by how my own expectations of what must be normal interfere. Last week in the car, for example, Vita decided to read Ishmael some fairy tales to pass the time. I hadn't heard her read aloud for years, maybe not since she was six or seven, yet now she read easily and expressively. "Hey," I thought, "don't you have to *practice* reading aloud before you can read like that?" I thought this to myself — I didn't say a word — and yet simply thinking it, simply having assumed that Vita must not be good at reading aloud because she never practiced, must surely have colored my view of her, and not just as a reader, but as a competent person.

In a fury, while Vita continued with the fairy tale and Ishmael blithely listened, I remembered back to my own childhood, and how my teachers always pushed us to practice reading aloud. Yet when we *did* practice, it was during our reading group, on the spot in front of seven or eight other kids (plus an unknown quantity of bored kids in the rest of the classroom struggling with their mimeographed work-sheets), all listening, as the teacher was, for every mistake that we might make. None of us ever read aloud as lyrically as Vita was now doing, and yet I suppose we bought into the whole idea that practice was necessary precisely because we kept stumbling over the words. Only now, years later, did I realize that we stumbled because we had been too scared to do anything else. Practice or no practice had nothing to do with it.

Ishmael says that in his everyday life, he knows that he is still reacting to the effects of school. This surprises me, since he spent little more than a year in school and has almost no memory of it. Yet it takes kids almost no time at all, once they go to school, to learn just what skills, knowledge, and methods of learning the school establishment values. School values have become such a powerful instrument in our culture, and hence in our imagination, that once we become aware of them we can never simply ignore them. We spend the rest of our lives reacting to them, either by choosing to be mainstream and complying with them or by defying them in various ways and to varying degrees. Ishmael, I imagine, still finds himself making choices, at least to some degree, based on compliance or defiance.

As for me, I am amazed at how many conventional assumptions about how all children learn I have still never questioned. It is these assumptions — "Children will never learn to read aloud unless they practice," or "Children need to be taught the correct way to shape each letter or they'll never learn to write efficiently" — that, when put into practice, interfere with children's real work.

When Ishmael turned out to be a born speller — he could spell "elephant" by the time he was five — I smiled happily at him the way I smile at Vita when I catch her in bed in the wee hours of the morning reading *Little Women*. I know that these are not activities that all children enjoy or do at the same ages as Vita and Ishmael, but to me that doesn't matter. Clearly, I feel comfortable with their differences, here, their unique ways of learning. When Vita showed no interest in spelling correctly, though, and not just at five, but at six and seven, I immediately stopped feeling comfortable with her *difference* (her uniqueness), because questions of what is normal for *all* children blurred my sight. I am still too quick to pull out the spellers, to want to patch up the differences. In doing this, I not only shut myself off from insights into the true process of my children's learning, but I threaten to shut them off as well. Like the parents at the zoo, every time I bring out the speller I am saying to my children, "It's the caged animals that are the important thing here, not the trampled popcorn." Said once too often, it will make them lose sight of the popcorn completely.

Perhaps it is the curse of motherhood to worry continually that we could have done better, to think that we ought to have done this or ought to have done that — to feel that we can never do enough. John Holt always said, "It's never too late." He's right, and yet to a mother, that is usually small comfort. "I've just read your article 'Living With Children' in *Mothering*," a grandmother wrote to me, "and I am crying because your focus on the children's feelings and respect for them as unique persons is what I didn't...give to my children." Would she have believed me if I had told her that I shed the same tears? And yet what continually amazes me is the trust my own children put in me — the trust that I *will* eventually learn.

As I have said, most children learn to mistrust their own learning process when they are faced with adults who mistrust it. In first grade, six-year-old Ishmael was different. Did he simply trust his teacher to learn about the way he worked the way he trusted me to do the same

11

thing? I don't know, but for whatever reasons, he didn't, or couldn't, abandon his own process despite the fact that he clearly wanted to please the teacher and I encouraged him to do so. Although he entered school able to read any word put before him, the teacher insisted that he learn to read all over again, this time using a standard phonetic system. He couldn't — something deep down inside wouldn't let him — do it. When the teacher told the children that they could take a ten from the tens column and turn it into ten ones in the ones column, Ishmael wouldn't, once again simply couldn't, believe her.

Describing the way children go about trying to make sense of the world around them, Seymour Papert wrote in his book *Mindstorms*, "Children do not follow a learning path that goes from one 'true position' to another more advanced 'true position.' Their natural learning paths include 'false theories' that teach us as much about theory building as true ones."

Perhaps because Ishmael's own "unorthodox ways of exploring the world" (especially in areas that overlapped with his schoolwork) were so highly developed and had already worked so well for him by the time he entered school, he just naturally clung even to his false theories, rather than blindly transferring his trust to his teacher. Yet it's not as if he didn't suffer.

"I had to stand up against the wall at recess again," Ishmael used to come home and tell me. "I *know* that I'm not supposed to read ahead in my reading book, but when there's nothing else to do I forget." Once he told me tearfully, "I had to sit in the back of the class and do a worksheet on suffixes and prefixes while everyone else had music. I didn't finish when I was supposed to, but that was because when I'm just reading words to myself I read the whole word. I can't see all the little parts unless Mrs. R. shows them to me. I don't know why."

"I remember sitting at my desk trying to work out the answer to a math problem," Ishmael recalls now, "but I couldn't remember what I was supposed to be doing because none of it made any sense. It was very hot and stuffy. Most of the kids were already done with their work and were making noise. The boy next to me was running a little toy racing car up and down his desk. The more I tried to concentrate the hotter it seemed, and the noise made my head hurt terribly."

One day the teacher called me in, agitated and distressed, because she was sure that Ishmael didn't know his colors. "I gave the children a work sheet with a variety of geometrical shapes on it and I asked them to color them in, as neatly as they possibly could. I told them to color the circle red, the triangle green, the rectangle blue and so on, but look," and here she produced Ishmael's paper, "all he did was color in part of the triangle."

Later, she worried that he might have a learning disability. "He reads all right," she said, "but when I ask him to summarize what he reads he can't do it. Instead, he recounts the stories practically word for word. I think he has trouble grasping whole concepts. What I'd like to recommend is that we have him tested by a trained specialist. It's worth it, you know, to catch these things early on."

At school, it became a real problem when Ishmael took ten or fifteen minutes to zip up his jacket and put on his mittens. "By that time recess is already over," his frustrated teacher pointed out. For me, though, the really frustrating thing was that at home, Ishmael seemed to be supremely competent. At six, he read *The Wind in the Willows*. He pulled his baby rocking chair up to his toy box, making a desk for himself, and wrote "books." His concentration was intense as he placed the last block on his already swaying four-foot- high block tower or climbed to the very tip-top of the old apple tree. I saw these things and told the teacher about them but the question she always raised was, "Why isn't Ishmael competent in school?" She never asked, "Why is he so competent at home?"

It was surely that early competence that gave us the courage to teach Ishmael at home in the first place. "He may not be able to summarize a story in a few words," I remember Bob saying, "but he has such a wonderful way of lingering over details and fine points! Obviously he understands everything he reads. What more could the teacher possibly want?" What we didn't understand at the time, though, any more than the teacher did, was that Ishmael was competent at home simply because, by taking his activities as seriously as we took our own work, we allowed him to think of himself as a competent person. It wasn't as if we consciously considered his activities (or Vita's) serious work from the start, though. We had to learn and Vita and Ishmael were insistent teachers.

For the longest time, for example, it never occurred to me that when I needed to go to the store, I shouldn't simply call to the kids and ask them to get ready — pronto. Although I never would have called them bad or stubborn, I used to be caught off guard each time by their sudden bursts of tears and vociferous objections. Did it never occur to me, in advance, that they might be legitimately busy — that they might have work to do that couldn't stand to be interrupted without warning? What they showed me, though, as I walked into their room all set to hush and reason with them, always left me feeling abashed.

Perhaps I found an elaborate military set-up, "the little people and the acorns pitched for battle," as Ishmael would have explained it, and the fate of the good queen still uncertain, or Vita in the middle of painstakingly typing out one of her three-line stories. Perhaps one of Vita and Ishmael's block towers had just tumbled to the ground and they were now feverishly rebuilding it. Wouldn't I have protested, too, at being interrupted under similar circumstances? *Didn't* I protest just as loudly when one of them interrupted me in the middle of a sentence I was struggling to write to ask me to reach up to the high shelf for the bag of raisins? I hope I always had the presence of mind to apologize to them when I so rudely interrupted their work the way they always apologized to me.

My friend Dick Furnas, who is a math teacher, once told me that in trying to understand why his students come up with certain answers, he always assumes, first, that their answers are correct. "That is, I try to understand where my students are coming from," he said, "by discovering a context in which their answers *could* make sense."

As I sat on the floor with Vita and Ishmael, drying their tears and watching their games, I often thought with a kind of terror, "And this is what I almost destroyed!" As with Dick and his students, I was learning (but never fast enough) that *within the context of their own play,* Vita's and Ishmael's tears made a great deal of sense.

In time I did learn to plan my trips to the store with the kids well in advance; to bring washcloths and toothbrushes *to them,* when necessary, rather than insisting that they run to the bathroom to clean up; and to give them plenty of notice before mealtimes. The more I got to know their play the more I came to admire and delight in it and to see its importance. They, more than anything, showed me exactly what Bruno Bettelheim meant when he wrote:

> Besides being a means of coping with past and present concerns, play is the child's most useful tool for preparing himself for the future and its tasks.... A child at play begins to realize that he need not give up in despair if a block doesn't balance neatly on another block the first time around. Fascinated by the challenge of building a tower, he

gradually learns that even if he doesn't succeed immediately, success can be his if he perseveres. He learns not to give up at the first sign of failure, or at the fifth or tenth, and not to turn in dismay to something less difficult, but to try again and again." (*Atlantic Monthly*, March 1987)

Giving Vita and Ishmael plenty of warning before we had to go to the store avoided a lot of unnecessary nagging and unpleasantness, of course, but more important, it gave them the message that we took their play seriously — that we now recognized it as a kind of work, just as worthwhile as our own. Vita and Ishmael, in turn, not only continued to take pride in their games and creations, but they never lost the feeling of ownership or trust in the process of their creation that they had had when they were babies.

Children, I gradually discovered under Vita and Ishmael's tutelage, will never learn self-discipline as a skill separate from the work they perceive *as their real work.*

Yet it is this real work that schools inadvertently steal from children, as the teacher tried to do when she told Ishmael that he had to learn how to read all over again using *her* phonetic system, or learn how to subtract using *her* rules (no matter how sensible!).

In a recent letter, Susannah Sheffer wrote, "My eighth grade teacher, if you can believe it, said, 'Use dashes when you're *your own author*, never for me!',", implying, of course, that when Susannah and her classmates wrote school assignments they were not "their own authors," but the teacher's. Some children, like Ishmael, go through any amount of suffering to hold onto and protect their work in school. Others simply allow it to be lost.

I think of Vita, who normally spends several hours every day cutting, pasting, molding clay or folding paper in the art room. Yet she automatically stops working on art at home when she goes to even the nicest art class for any length of time. Not only does she stop "making things" at home, but she manages to do the most slap-dash and uninspired work in class. I think of myself, who only started to read and write seriously after I left school, and even of one of my favorite writers, V.S. Naipaul, who (dare I say "like me"?) only began writing after he, too, had left school behind him.

I do not really know how I came to be a writer. I can give certain dates and certain facts about my career. But the process remains mysterious. It is mysterious, for instance, that the ambition should have come first — the wish to be a writer, to have that distinction, that fame — and that this ambition should have come long before I could think of anything to write about.

I remember, in my first term at Oxford in 1950, going for long walks — I remember the roads, the autumn leaves, the cars and trucks going by, whipping the leaves up — and wondering what I was going to write about. I had worked hard for the scholarship to go to Oxford, to be a writer. But now that I was in Oxford, I didn't know what to write about. (*New York Review of Books*, April 23, 1987)

Perhaps for Vita and me, and even for V.S. Naipaul, by "losing" our work, by delaying it until we were free of the classroom (in Vita's case, the art classroom), we were, like Ishmael, simply protecting it. Yet most people seem to think that this process of delaying one's work is a healthy one and that it is unnatural, even bad, for children to find a focus for their work at an early age.

People often say disparagingly of prodigies, the only children we usually think of as having "work" in the first place, that "They may be remarkable when they're young, but they always go through a period of mental crisis later, when they discover that they have to rethink everything that they once did unconsciously. Just look at Yehudi Menuhin."

And as Menuhin said himself in his autobiography, "Considering that I played without thinking, without analysis, without, as it were, taking the machine apart for overhaul, just keeping it running at any cost, my performance stood up remarkably well; but there were times when I knew I wouldn't be able to go on until I understood technique and could recapture that ease I had once possessed without thinking and which was now deserting me."

Yehudi Menuhin *did* go through a very rough time, yet I think that what this passage makes so clear, and what is so important about it, is not that he was on the verge of a mental crisis, but that *all along* he was allowed to *own* his own work. He grew up trusting himself to create his own systems for pursuing his work and always took responsibility for it, even when that involved a sometimes painful struggle.

By way of contrast, Susannah was only free to articulate how she works best when she was twenty-two and just out of college. She wrote then, "I can write a poem in a train station or in a crowded office, but I can't do it and listen to music at the same time. I think that to listen to the poem's rhythm, I can't have another rhythm getting in the way.

But I very often 'get' poems, that is, receive the initial inspiration, while listening to symphony orchestras or watching ballet.... While watching or listening to unworded things, the word part of me is distracted and is able to be caught unawares, which creates that state of receptivity that is necessary for writing poems."

Vita, meanwhile, at age eleven, is already able to understand the way she works well enough to explain that, "At first I had no idea why I lost interest in art when I took art classes. But now I know that what I like best about art is figuring things out — taking little boxes apart to see how they are made, for example, and then making my own — or experimenting with elaborate cut-outs, overlays, and paper springs when I make birthday cards. In the art classes, though, I hated it when my teachers expected me to make everything their way. In fact, I hated it so much that for a long time afterwards, I hated thinking about art at all."

At fifteen, Ishmael too is beginning to understand and articulate how he works as an artist. "No, I never feel that way," he said recently in response to a reporter who described Van Cliburn as saying, "When I perform I feel an incredible sense of power over my audiences because no matter how well or poorly I play, they always enjoy it."

"I feel a sense of power, too, but it's over the instrument," Ishmael went on to explain. "It's the exhilaration of making even just one note sound on the piano in a way that I didn't think possible."

Thinking about how he works helps him to discover what it is he needs to learn and to formulate appropriate questions to help seek out the necessary answers. "I've always wanted to know what it is like to play the same full recital on two consecutive nights," he recently confessed to a professional pianist who was still dripping with sweat from a performance.

"It's like scrutinizing the music with a magnifying glass," the pianist said. "Ah," I could see Ishmael thinking, as if in instant recognition, his sense of the work still so perfectly intact.

A few weeks ago I sat for a couple of hours watching Ishmael practice Beethoven's "Waldstein" sonata. He worked on relaxation — dropping his hand so that his fingers fell into the keys without making harsh sound. He practiced lifting off notes so that his silences were clean but not abrupt. He practiced loud passages, cutting away, instantly, to almost nothing. Ishmael worked lovingly, as if time had no meaning, as if each note, each phrase and each break in sound — each silence — was a pearl worth polishing. For me, totally absorbed in Ishmael's work, there was an overwhelming feeling of exhilaration.

Then, suddenly, as if shaken rudely out of sleep, I realized, "*This is what Ishmael's first grade teacher would have stolen from him if he had let her!*" It wasn't just that she was determined to teach him a new way to read or to do speed drills in math or to summarize stories, but that by blindly pursuing her conventional assumptions about how children ought to learn, she had failed to see, to *really* see and appreciate, the context within which Ishmael's unique way of learning made sense. Out of sheer blindness, she had unwittingly tried to teach him to mistrust and even abandon the incredible devotion to detail and the determination to stretch out every second that were already forming the very essence of his intelligence and creative capacity. Thank God Ishmael never gave up on me, but insisted that I learn to look closely enough so that I couldn't steal it either.

Trusting
the Process

"Remember when Vita played us her Debussy this morning," my mother said, "and she repeated the first section twice?"

"Oh, yes, because I asked her to," I said, feeling embarrassed. "I knew she could play it better."

"But, no," my mother answered. "She *wanted* to play it again. Anyone could see that she wanted to get it right, even though it wasn't going to be fun to play it again." My mother was vehement. "*That's* what I mean by rigor. No school could have taught her that!"

It is all too easy to accustom ourselves to the everyday attitudes toward authority, professionalism, and expertise that most of us first develop in school, or to forget how easily we still lose confidence in ourselves in the face of those attitudes. Occasionally we are shocked into remembering.

Last year, for example, Vita had an operation to stem internal bleeding caused, they later told us, by a rare birth defect. Perfectly healthy until the bleeding started — rosy-cheeked and energetic — she turned paler and paler over a period of several days until, ghost-like, she fell unconscious on the bathroom floor. As we carried her into the emergency room the faces of the hospital staff reflected the fear we felt. Never have I seen so many doctors appear so fast. Nurses hovered over Vita, set to go into action.

Yet before I could even help to undress Vita the woman from the front desk showed up. "Come with me," she said with a voice all sympathy. "I need to get your billing and insurance information."

"But we can't possibly leave Vita," I told her. My steadfastness surprised me, yet already I could feel myself weakening.

"Don't worry," the woman said, "Vita is in the hands of professionals. There is nothing more you can do." She turned to leave, as if sure we were going to follow.

Then a nurse turned to me. "Why don't you get a cup of coffee?" she suggested. "You're going to need to look after yourselves, too, you know."

An aide wheeled Vita into the X-ray room. Bob and I hesitantly followed. They stood Vita up on the tile floor and pushed her chest against the X-ray machine. Bob barely managed to catch her as she collapsed, once again unconscious. I was furious at the hospital, but even more furious at myself. Even I had begun to believe that I was merely in the way of the hospital staff. It took Vita to remind me that I was still needed — still a mother.

During the next two days they gave her tests. Rarely did they allow us to stay with her. Only in the hallways, as they wheeled her from test to test, could we comfort her. We knew, of course, how desperately she needed us to be with her, and yet we passively gave in to the hospital rules and regulations. We didn't once raise a major fuss.

On the afternoon of the second day they operated. When the doctor came out of the operating room three hours later he was exhausted. "We finally found it," he said. "She'll be fine now." Then he fell into a chair. "You folks were really great throughout this ordeal. I know just how traumatic something like this can be."

The doctor was sympathetic to us, and his expertise had indeed saved Vita's life. Yet I knew that he was really just showing his appreciation for the way we had quickly learned to stand back and let him do his job. His competence and expertise depended on our staying out of the way. For this reason, in the hospital I lost faith in my own competence.

"But Nancy," friends are quick to point out, "You know as well as anybody that *you* couldn't have operated on Vita." True. And yet I don't believe that just because the doctor had skills we lacked, and was able at that moment to help Vita in ways we could not, an unequal relationship was the only one available to us. In a different system, and with a different attitude, the doctor might have involved me as a responsible partner. He might have seen that while he knew some things about Vita that I did not (what might be wrong with her in medical terms, and how to operate on her), I knew other things about her that *he* did not (what she was likely to be feeling, how to reassure her and make her comfortable, and so on). If the doctor had recognized this instead of excluding me, I might have been able to benefit from his skill and competence without letting my own be undermined.

Unfortunately most schools, where the traditional teacher/student relationship prevails, are no different from hospitals, or any institution, for that matter, based on the inequality inherent in a professional/client relationship. From the time they enter school, children are expected to submit to the supposedly greater competence and authority of their teachers rather than encouraged to use their teachers' skill and knowledge in whatever ways make sense to them. As a result, they quickly lose their independence and motivation and slip into the role of dependents, convinced by the very nature of the institution and by the attitudes of many of its teachers that in order to learn what is important they need classrooms, teachers, and textbooks. They grow so accustomed to the same feelings of helplessness and incompetence that I experienced in the hospital with Vita that they don't even notice their loss of autonomy. Nor do their teachers. On all sides it is simply taken for granted:

Students go to school to learn. Teachers go to school to teach them what they need to know.

Although there has been pressure, recently, to begin teaching even the youngest children to read and swim and perform other feats once reserved for much older children, babies, for the most part, are still left alone to guide their own learning process. Interestingly, although they show remarkable determination and perseverance, they are seldom — perhaps never — conscious of trying to learn things. Babies waking up in the morning do not grit their teeth and say to themselves, "Okay, I've practiced enough. Today I'll try to take my first steps." They don't think within any sort of given time frame. If they have an immediate need, they do what they can to satisfy it. Every day babies are able to be more precise with their language and physical motions, and yet they are unaware of the effort involved.

Gradually, though, the process shifts focus. Children, even as young as two or three, become aware that the bigger people around them know many things that they would like to know too. Consciously they begin to include us in their learning work.

"Why does the car start when you turn the key?" three-year-old Ishmael asked Bob from his car seat.

"Because it ignites the gasoline and air in the cylinder of the motor."

"Why?"

"Because that makes an explosion which makes the wheel turn."

"Why?" Ishmael asked again and again. "Why? Why? Why?"

Although we generally trust babies to learn everything crucial to their early development, we seldom think of the way they go about learning in terms of an organized process, simply because their learning seems so instinctive and unconscious. Even outside of a formal school setting, then, involving us in their learning work seems to me to demand remarkable courage on the part of children. So often, when they reach out to us for help, we take it as a ready invitation to create an organized process for them to follow — one that, because they do respect and depend on us to such a degree, they may feel they have no choice but to go along with.

Even though we may not intend it, when we do this we tend to turn children into passive receivers or demand that they become "empty containers," as John Holt put it, waiting and ready for us to fill. Too often the process involves molding children ("Go home and play this passage twenty-five times"), guiding them for what we determine is their own good ("Say 'thank you' to Mrs. Jones for giving you the cookies"), and even humoring them ("Good schools" give children math games to play rather than drilling them with flash cards.). Often, our attempts to bring order to children's learning are downright condescending.

"I can't talk to her," Ishmael wrote about one of his early piano teachers. "Her character is different from mine. I think she is silly, and she thinks that I am a glum person in need of cheering up or something and she tries exactly the wrong method. But it's not only that; she has a beastly habit of asking me things like, 'What is the most wonderful moment in the whole piece?' that put me on the spot and make me feel that there is *one* right answer and I have to find it — though she knows herself and ought to tell me, probably."

Similarly, Vita's orchestra conductor asks the kids rhetorical questions as a way to catch their interest. When they aren't playing loudly enough she asks, "What does *forte* mean?"

As if to verify her notion that they are incapable of thinking on their own, they answer with questions:

"Louder?"

"Play closer to the bridge?"

"Use arm weight?"

When we first took Ishmael out of school and I explained to a friend that I wanted him to love learning and never have to sit in a classroom hating the multiplication tables, she said, "Of course, you are going to try to make math fun for Ishmael."

My mother, more concerned with self-discipline than fun, asked, "But how will you teach him the meaning of rigor?"

"Wasn't Ishmael born knowing that?" I thought, remembering fondly baby Ishmael's rigorous attempts to pull on his snow boots in sub-zero weather to escape outside; his rigorous attempts to reach the phone or cookies cooling on the counter; and his determined looks as he tried to hammer and saw in the shed.

I was sure that I would never teach Ishmael in such a way as to make him unhappy and besides, he had already convinced us that he could learn most of the important things under his own steam. He had taught himself how to read and write, after all, and as I said before, he was a born speller. There were, of course, things that he didn't know — some things, in fact, that I was sure required teaching. It never for a moment occurred to me then, or for several more years, in fact, that by deciding to teach Ishmael skills that I was sure he would never pick up on his own — how to find common denominators, for example — I might actually interfere with his learning work — with the very rigor that my mother was talking about. Only much later would I realize that *any* time we decide to teach children the things we are sure they can't learn from experience in the real world, we not only remove them from the very world they are trying so hard to understand, by creating artificial learning situations for them, but we imply that they are incompetent learners and need to rely on our greater expertise and knowledge in order to learn properly.

If, in real life, it was as simple as merely answering children's questions when they asked, perhaps we would eventually abandon our pretense of authority and learn to respond to children on their own terms, the way we do when they are babies. Unfortunately, real life is not that simple. Sometimes, when children come to us for help, they have no clear questions. They want something, often very badly, and yet they aren't sure enough of what it is to be able to articulate it.

Justin, Vita's six-year-old violin student, provided me with a perfect, although occasionally agonizing, example of this, one that I wrote about for issue #68 of *Growing Without Schooling* with the title "The Relationship Between Learning and Teaching" (slightly revised here at Vita's and Justin's insistence):

> Surprisingly, since Vita is a violinist and pianist but not, like her brother Ishmael, a composer, her violin lessons with Justin have gradually turned into composition lessons. Sometimes Vita and Justin hardly play at all, but every week he brings in a fresh page of music, lovingly notated in red and blue ink.
>
> One day, when they were still going through the first Suzuki violin book piece by piece, Justin announced as Vita arrived at his lesson, "I can read music!" and he could. His mother had shown him that the printed notes on a page symbolize actual pitches that he could play on his violin, and she had pointed out that by memorizing the location of just one note on the staff — in this case it was the G on the second line from the bottom — he could figure out the rest of the notes by interval.
>
> This knowledge seemed to give Justin an incredible sense of power. He no longer had to wait for people to teach him songs. He soon realized, though, that there was more to music-reading than just figuring out the notes that the composer wanted him to play, and he asked Vita plaintively, "How come when I play the right notes the piece *still* doesn't sound right?" "Well," she said, with more honesty than diplomacy, "You are going to have to learn to read rhythm, too."

Like many children who have learned to read words by writing them, Justin apparently needed to write music down in order to really understand it. He began writing many different kinds of notes, as if that was the only way that he could clarify for himself the different rhythmic quantities that notes represent. The act of writing them down set them firmly in his mind, more firmly than any teacher could have instilled them in him with the usual method of making him clap out rhythms. After that, every time he learned a new technique on the violin he asked Vita to write it. Justin was now writing page after page of music, and yet in his own mind, and certainly in Vita's, he was still a violinist — a violinist busily learning as much as he could about how to read music.

Perhaps Justin trusted all along that Vita would be able to teach him the things he felt he needed to know in order to become a composer. Maybe that's why, after the initial excitement over note-reading wore off, he still patiently unpacked his violin and played for her each week, even though we could all sense that he was itching for something else to happen. But what? Justin didn't seem to know, and for several weeks it seemed as if all he could do was wait, and keep asking his questions, until he became conscious enough of what he really wanted to be able to ask Vita for it in words.

Meanwhile, I found myself wondering if Justin's questions weren't merely symptoms of frustration. Perhaps, I thought, he was using them as a stalling tactic, a way to avoid telling Vita that he had lost interest in the violin altogether. Vita offered no theories of her own, but she, too, was obviously troubled by the way things were going. Yet when, as so often happened, Justin set down his violin in the middle of playing a piece to ask Vita a question like how to write stems on quarter notes, she always told him immediately. Neither Vita nor Justin realized why he was more interested in stemming notes than in playing nice pieces. Vita worried that she wasn't giving Justin what he really needed, and I know she worried that one day he might stop coming to lessons.

Fortunately, Vita kept answering Justin's questions the minute he asked them, even when that meant interrupting the music they were playing. Justin kept coming to lessons, and one day he brought the beginnings of a real piece with him. After that, he arrived each week with new drafts and new additions. Rather than interrupting the main business of the lesson — violin — the piece seemed to complement it, since in order to revise and correct it, which is what Justin wanted, they needed to play it over and over again. The piece was, in many ways, a journal of everything Justin was learning to play, and I noticed that in order to develop more ideas for the piece, he had begun to play more.

It certainly wasn't the typically tuneful piece you would expect a child to write. There is no way you can hum it the way you might hum

"Mary Had a Little Lamb." In fact, there are only a few real melodies in the piece, perhaps because Justin was primarily concerned with exploring all of the technical possibilities of violin playing and notation. Sometimes, watching this young boy hand Vita the latest addition to his piece, I was tempted to wonder if he was concerned with anything *beyond* constructing a random hodgepodge of technical "fireworks." But each week Justin made it clear that he had definite ideas about where he wanted the piece to go and how he wanted it to sound.

"Play that," he often said to Vita as he set his music on the stand. When she did, he might then single out a measure and say, "But I wanted it to slow down there."

"Oh," she'd say. "Shall we add a ritard?"

"Does that mean 'slow down'?" Vita would nod yes. "Good," he'd say. "How do you write it?" (This is a kid, I kept reminding myself, who can barely read!)

It never once occurred to Vita to doubt the legitimacy of Justin's interest in or ability for composing, but now that they were working so intensely on the piece, I think she even stopped noticing if Justin forgot to unpack his violin at the beginning of his lesson. And it was almost without thinking that she finally put a label on what he was doing. "Did you compose more during the week?" she asked one day as he walked in the door, rather than greeting him with the usual, "What did you *write* this week?"

Almost imperceptibly Justin had again taken control of the lessons. His mind no longer seemed to wander, he no longer itched with obvious frustration. And yet it seemed to me that it was only when he heard the word "compose" ascribed to his week's work that he (and Vita) became conscious of the change that had taken place.

Where another teacher might have been disappointed because Justin now openly preferred composing music to playing it, Vita wasn't disappointed at all. She had been willing to live with confusion and frustration rather than doubt Justin, but now she was simply relieved that he was so clear about the work he wanted to do and the ways in which she could help.

Susannah Sheffer responded by writing:

Your story says so much about learning and teaching, and, interestingly, about their interdependence. In the traditional teaching model, the whole question of whether Justin was there to learn to play the violin or to write music would have been in an important sense up to Vita. If she saw herself as a violin teacher only, she might not have had the interest or the patience to wait out the gradual but significant shift in Justin's priorities. She might well have said, "I offered to teach violin; if you want something else, you'll have to look elsewhere for it." I don't think she would necessarily have been to blame if she had said this — we can't make people teach what they don't want to teach any more than we can make people learn what they don't want to learn. But it would have made things different for Justin.

If, on the other hand, Vita had been willing to teach Justin whatever he wanted to learn, but had been too uncomfortable during the period of ambiguity and frustration to allow it to resolve itself *by* itself, she might have jumped in and decided to teach composition before Justin was sure that that was what he was asking of her. "Justin's interest in the violin is flagging," she might have thought to herself. "I'll have to do something to keep him interested in lessons."

Neither of these things *is* what happened, and I'm thinking of yet a third thing that might have happened but didn't. Justin might have decided to go it completely alone, thinking to himself that Vita was no longer giving him exactly what he wanted (even if he couldn't yet articulate what he did want). He might have stopped taking lessons soon after he began to feel vaguely dissatisfied, and then — well, I don't know what would have happened then. Certainly he might have figured out, at some time and in some way, that composition was what he really wanted to do. But what fascinates me, in your story, is how Justin was able to figure this out *with* Vita's help. I'm interested in how their sticking together through this somewhat confused time helped Justin discover what he most wanted from Vita, and Vita discover how she could best give it to him.

Clearly, Vita was able to trust Justin throughout his struggle, and likewise, to trust the *process* of the struggle itself, because being so close to her own childhood allowed her to understand that the struggle was necessary, but the resolution inevitable. Justin, too, trusted Vita to be sure of this, even though there must have been times when he wasn't so sure himself. Often, though, despite their internal itchings and near explosions, children can't trust us, and they hold back. They need to wait before they come to us for help until they are sure enough about what they need to be confident of protecting their work and methods for exploration from our temptation to take over the process for them.

At times like this it is especially hard for us to wait. When we do, we are often surprised by how quickly our children learn. I think again of Justin announcing to Vita that his mother had taught him to read music. How many music teachers would have believed it possible for a child as young as Justin to learn so fast? Perhaps it was only possible, though, because by holding back, waiting, Justin had been able, unconsciously, to figure out how the notes on a staff translated into music before he ever went to his mother for help. It wasn't so much that she taught him to read music, then, but that she helped raise his unconscious understanding to consciousness.

In my own mind, as a way to think about this and make sense of it, I often go back to the way Vita and Ishmael memorize piano pieces. Crazy as this may sound, they never decide to start memory work until on some deep level they are already sure that the piece is memorized. The act of memorizing, for them, like the act of "learning to read music" for Justin, means filling in a few blanks — making sure of a measure here or a note there — and most important, gaining enough conscious understanding of the music so they can feel confident of not losing it. Whereas once their fingers might have been able to lead them through the piece, now their own minds actively know where they are and which notes and phrases come next.

In his new book, *Learning All the Time*, John Holt says that although many math books try to explain why multiplication works the way it does by saying that multiplication is distributive over addition, "to most people this won't be very helpful.... The question 'Why is it so?'," he writes, "does not make any more sense than asking why it is that we can split a group of 7 objects into a group of 3 objects and a group of 4 objects. It is so because that's what happens. There isn't some other deeper truth hiding behind that truth." And he then says, "Perhaps if we see clearly enough that what I have been writing about *is* just a fact of nature, we may not need an explanation."

At first, this seemed to me to be a cop out. I thought of Ishmael in first grade, struggling with the concept of borrowing. But then I realized that the reason he had so much trouble accepting the teacher's explanation of why borrowing works the way it does is that he hadn't already figured it out for himself. If he had, even if his knowledge had been buried deep in his unconscious the way his piano pieces initially are or Justin's knowledge of note-reading must have been, he would certainly have surprised the teacher by his skill at learning — his aptitude and intelligence. As it was, Ishmael seemed to her to be frustratingly slow. If only she could have had the patience or the trust (not to mention the freedom to stray from the required curriculum) to wait until Ishmael's answers were already in place, ready to be brought into consciousness.

Yet how do we tell when children are really ready for our help, especially when we can feel them itching and even exploding inside, as I often did with Justin? How can we be sure not to exert our authority, the way Vita's doctor did with me, and undermine their belief in their own competence, their own ability to make paths into the world? There are no easy answers. "Figuring out how you can be most helpful to learners who are at the same time figuring out what they want to learn and how you can help them is not the same as deciding what you will teach and then teaching it," Susannah wrote at the end of her response to my story about Justin, "but it is not *nothing*, either.... Vita was part of Justin's process of discovery in a hundred ways, most of which we'll probably never know." Whatever you do, she was saying, stay involved, keep searching for answers, don't give up.

CHAPTER

Musicians at Work

> The way in which man can find his own place is to tune his instrument to the keynote of the chord to which he belongs.
> — Hazrat Inuyat Khan in *The Music of Life*

Vita and Ishmael now spend most of each working day playing and composing music. Aside from the sheer glory of doing my own work to the melodic strains of Chopin ballades, Beethoven sonatas, and Bach preludes and fugues, living with Vita and Ishmael's music and being as involved as I am in their musical work has meant that of everything they do, it is the way they approach music that I understand and know most intimately. Often, I find myself using this understanding as a base or guidepost for looking at how they work on everything else in life. Watching the way Vita explores a new piece on the violin or piano, for example, teaches me about how she explores spelling or numerical relationships or art. By learning as much as I can about how she learns music, I can begin to learn about the ways that I, like she with Justin, can be a part of her process of discovery — how I can be useful to her as she pursues her work.

Needless to say, I have made more mistakes, as a teacher, with music, than with anything else I have worked on with Vita and Ishmael. But despite the mistakes, some of which have verged on the disastrous, Vita and Ishmael have watched me learn to care so deeply about music that they have never even thought to exclude me from their learning work. They have shown me how, even when they share the same piano bench for a whole afternoon, they are never tempted to compromise their own individual viewpoints. They have shown me how, at the same time, they feel free to experiment with and even change their approaches to learning music as their viewpoints shift or change focus.

When Vita was almost five and Ishmael eight, they began studying the piano. She was already a dancer; he was a singer. That is, Vita never walked, she danced from place to place, whereas Ishmael stumbled along, humming to himself with every step. For the longest time, that difference between them seemed to me to be the crucial one. Every time Vita sat down at the piano, her fingers danced across the keys the way her feet danced. Her gestures were so nimble and rhythmic. Yet at four and a half, she wasn't the least concerned about playing the proper notes. Ishmael, on the other hand, sang at the piano. Quite literally, he sang as he played, and he cared deeply about making the notes sing. The trouble was — and this persisted for a long time — his fingers stumbled on the keys the way his feet stumbled when he walked. By the time he was able to play real pieces — a Clementi sonatina, for example — we used to laugh and say, "When you make your debut in Carnegie Hall you'll have to bring Vita along to play the trills!"

As time went by, Ishmael learned to trill and to play fast running passages, arpeggios, and double thirds and Vita decided that playing the notes in the same order that the composer wrote them was important. But already, another major difference had emerged. Ishmael was glued to the piano. Once his fingers learned to travel the keyboard he seemed content never to look at another instrument. When my grandmother said, "The piano gives you every instrument of the orchestra to play with," he knew exactly what she meant. He listened for the violins and clarinets in the sounds of the notes he played, and unlike me, he heard them. He felt no need to look further than the piano keyboard.

By then, Ishmael had emerged as a serious composer, but that too seemed to be a natural extension of his work at the piano. Not only did the piano give him his orchestra, but it gave him the physical means to play and improvise around the tunes he heard non-stop in his mind. Once he discovered music paper, it made perfect sense to him to write his improvisations down and to extend and organize them with his pencil as well as his fingertips.

Meanwhile, Vita, who was just as passionate a musician as Ishmael, never seemed to be as sharply focused. She had only played the piano for about six months, for example, when she stood up in her chair at a concert, pointed to a violin, and said, "I want to play THAT!" She was sure there was nothing more beautiful than a polished violin and with her, aesthetics made all the difference. To her dismay, though, she all too soon realized that to make a beautiful sound on the instrument was quite a struggle. She persevered and yet, perhaps as a way to balance her difficulties with the violin, she began experimenting with harmonicas, recorders, and pennywhistles. "Will it be the tuba tomorrow?" I used to wonder. When she was old enough she joined a chorus and became an enthusiastic and disciplined singer. And, as she wrote in her diary, she began composing songs for the chorus to perform.

Despite the multiple forms that her interest in music takes, Vita, like Ishmael, now plays serious pieces with technical security and understanding. It's no wonder, since both kids spend most of their waking hours making music of one kind or another. Even when we go on trips Vita and Ishmael bring their music with them. Vita, of course, can take most of her instruments along. Ishmael travels with music paper and sharpened pencils, although that never seems quite satisfactory. Once, when our family was visiting my mother, she exclaimed, "Look, Ishmael is playing the washing machine!" And sure enough, there he was, three thousand miles away from home and his piano, banging out rhythms with a pair of drum sticks and knocking his knees into her machine for occasional added resonance.

Music is obviously central to Vita and Ishmael's relationship as well as to their lives. Yet although they have been living together and sharing their music for years now, they continue to hear and feel music, to express it, and even to go about learning it in the first place, very differently. Vita approaches music and absorbs it in every way *but* as a musician — as a storyteller, as an actress, as a dancer, and especially as an artist — whereas Ishmael goes directly into the deepest recesses of the music itself, as a listener, a pianist, and a composer. This, of course, is simply a subtle extension of their initial musical choices — Ishmael, the totally focused pianist; Vita, the multiple personality. Oddly, although I lived day in and day out with the kids' music-making and could feel the difference in their approaches, it was only thanks to Ishmael's composition teacher that I learned to articulate the difference. What I needed was a whole new musical vocabulary, and he was the one, through Ishmael, who first offered it to me.

During their first lesson Stephen May asked, "What do you have to show me?" Ishmael, who was then eleven, shyly took out his "Literary Symphony." Stephen scanned Ishmael's lovingly penciled pages for what seemed to me to take forever and a day. Then, turning to Ishmael, he said severely, "Why are all of your textures the same? And you know you make absolutely no use of tone color." Then Stephen leaned back in his chair. "You'd better start out by writing in smaller forms," he said. "I'll give you some exercises to do for next week." Ishmael nodded (undaunted, I should add), although like me, I don't think that he had ever heard of "texture" or "tone color" or even "form" — at least not as they related to music. Visual art, yes. But music?

Well, it wasn't long before Ishmael began using those terms as if they had been part of his earliest vocabulary. Over meals, or while he and Vita brushed their teeth, he liked to think out his composition "homework." "Stephen wants me to write a piano piece for next week that has some fixed order of sections — like an ABA, for instance. But the thing is, what I have to do is make certain that each section has a contrasting texture. That'll make it much easier for the audience to tell what is going on, you know. I don't really know what I'll do yet. Maybe I'll give the 'A' section a very simple rhythm and then write a rhythm in the 'B' section that's much more complex."

"Or maybe," he might muse, "I could write a first section with the texture divided into a melody and its accompaniment and then give the second section several different melodies that would go on at once. What would be really neat, though, would be to try to make some difference in tone color. I mean, if I was writing an orchestral piece I could give the 'A' section to the strings, perhaps, and the 'B' section to a group of contrasting instruments like the woodwinds. But with only a piano...well, it's something to think about, anyway."

From week to week Ishmael filled the house with those abstract terms, which, of course, lent themselves so perfectly to his abstract musing about composition (or perhaps gave them a concreteness that I couldn't yet fathom). But in any case, it was Vita who eventually illustrated them for me and helped me to see their significance in terms of the ways that both she and Ishmael approached and absorbed music. I used to sit with her every morning as she practiced, and one day (perhaps as a musical exercise for myself) I tried to listen to her music not as sound, but in terms of its bare-bones structure, the way Ishmael was now obviously thinking about music. That is, I tried to listen for the textures in the music she was playing, the tone colors, and the form. "I'm never going to be able to do this," I thought, "unless I look through the eyes of an artist *as well as* a musician." And then it hit me. That's just what Vita did! At least when she's inspired, she actually turns the notes and phrases of her music into pictures in her mind in order to make sense of them.

Color had always drawn Vita into the natural and human world. She thought of people in terms of the colors they wore and the colors they somehow exuded. She used colors dramatically in her artwork. Now, thinking about Vita as a "painter of music," I saw that as with color in art, by drawing out the color in her music — choosing to play a passage entirely on the lowest string of her violin to create a deep, rich (dark red) sound, for example, rather than simply crossing over to a higher string, or brushing her bow across the strings, well over on the fingerboard, to make a light, airy sound ("like very white puffy clouds drifting across a deep blue sky") — she made it accessible to herself, both emotionally and intellectually.

Watching Vita's face when she played music, it now occurred to me, was much like watching her face as she worked in the art room. The simplicity of her line drawings and water colors often seemed to me to reflect her own simplicity and clarity of feeling, whereas sometimes, as she worked cloth, paper, and bits of plastic into a collage, there was a complexity about her look that reminded me of the very textures that she was creating. The same was true with music. Brow furrowed, face set in total concentration, she would weave together the several strands of melody and harmony in a short but complex piece by Schumann, brightening up instantly, eyes glittering as if filled with visions of ballrooms, as she played the single line melody and simple oom-pa-pa harmony in the next piece.

Unlike Ishmael, who was immediately possessed by the idea of formal structure in music (once Stephen May helped him to become conscious of it), Vita never showed much interest in analyzing what she played. Yet she just naturally shaped her phrases to make them speak or sing and took breaths between sections as if to say, "Prepare yourself. Now I am going to introduce you to a new character." If tone color and texture provided her with the raw materials (allowing her the means with which to sketch her characters), it must have been her instinctive feeling for form that allowed her to tie them together, drawing out meaning and emotion from the notes on the page the way artists add meaning to their brush strokes by giving their paintings an overall structure and form, or storytellers add coherence to their words by their use of sequence and timing.

My discoveries about Vita's music-making were, as I said, what gave me the access to the vocabulary that finally enabled me to articulate to myself the significance of Ishmael's fascination with musical form, and to appreciate (even though it had been staring me in the face for years) that it was the sheer beauty of the form itself (and hence, the *way* it tied color and texture together) that drew him into music. I now understood that for Ishmael, music without form was like language without grammar. To discover the form in a piece, for him, was to discover the essence of its language; to write music within a specific form or to develop new forms was to give significance and meaning to isolated words and phrases.

As I thought about this my memories began to flow: I remembered how, long before he knew the form of a sonata, or a fugue or a rondo, Ishmael bounced up and down with excitement when we went to a concert and he heard a theme returning in a symphony or a chamber work. "Listen," he'd whisper, "that came at the beginning only this time the horns are playing it!"

His sense of phrasing seemed uncanny, even when he could barely read music. I remember sitting down at the piano, a month or two after we began taking lessons (yes, I wanted to learn how to play, too). Even though I had studied the viola for years as a child, I was absolutely stumped over a silly little folk song. I knew that I was playing the right notes because I'd checked them ten times over, and I was tapping hard enough with my foot so that I figured I couldn't help but have the rhythm right. And yet — the piece just didn't make sense!

Ishmael came up, noticing my frustration, and looked at the music over my shoulder. Then he asked if he could try it. It was a relief for me, actually, to give up my seat at the piano, but I listened with astonishment, as, on the first try (and without getting all the notes right by any means) he made the piece sound like real music.

"Well, you see," he said, pointing to the page, "You should have taken a breath here, where the phrase ends. Or didn't you notice that? And maybe you could have even lightened up a bit. Then the second phrase would have made more sense."

"Thanks," I said. "I'll try it."

At first, when Ishmael wrote music, the idea of musical form played no part — at least no conscious part. But when Stephen May mentioned form in that first composition lesson everything seemed to click. After that the whole way Ishmael went about composing changed. He still improvised at the piano and he still jotted down tunes (although mostly for reference), but when he actually sat down to compose a piece he now planned out the form before he ever decided what tunes he wanted to use.

Shortly after he began studying with Stephen, for example, he wrote a piece in rondeau form, "an ABABA as opposed to the Italian rondo form which is ABACA," Ishmael explained. "At least I think it's in rondeau form, even though the 'B' section returns in a slight variant."

More recently, when describing the first movement of his cello sonata, he wrote, "The first movement is a kind of combination of sonata-allegro and rondo form, schematized as ABAC-development-ACB. The section marked 'B' is at first only a fragment, but then it forms the main material of the development, which gets going at a great rate and pitches over into a very chaotic atonality."

Texture and tone color (ways of putting sounds and instruments together) became all the more important to him as he became concerned not only with form based on the melodic line (the horizontal form) but with vertical form — that is, form developed through the relations between the different musical parts that are layered together within a piece, such as harmony and counterpoint.

"I am now working on a piece for wind ensemble, piano, and bass," Ishmael wrote to a friend. "The main section of the piece is different textures and harmonies over a very slow theme in the bass, repeated four times, in the Japanese *in* scale."

Talking with Ishmael over meals about the pieces he was writing, reading the little notes he wrote to himself in the music he played ("sequence groups," "bass line important here"), and watching the look in his eyes when he and his piano teacher discovered hidden melodies and thematic variations, made it obvious to me that his approach to music was far more intellectual and analytical than Vita's. Yet he could be so moved by music that his response certainly seemed to be equally emotional.

Did the differences in their music making really matter that much if, in the end, they both played with heart and soul? I knew that it did when I first heard Ishmael's sonata for cello and piano performed and realized that whereas Vita painted and danced moods with her music, Ishmael was determined to convey ideas.

Ishmael talked about his sonata all during the months that he was writing it. We took brisk November walks together and he told me excitedly about the twelve-note chords he was developing and his plans for arranging the various sections. Later, before the perform-ance, I read (and reread and edited) his program notes.

"Because the kind of music I was writing started changing very quickly, I was faced with the problem of combining two virtually irreconcilable elements: modal tonality (which had been prominent in the first draft) and different kinds of highly chromatic harmony. I decided to make the 'subject' of the piece the struggle between these two styles."

In the third movement, as he said, "the conflict of styles is extended to become a conflict between instruments... a fierce rivalry." Then "things calm down, and both instruments in a sense have a vision of how they could be playing the movement in cooperation, in the form of a new theme (on a Japanese scale, although it does not sound particularly Oriental), played in canon. But alas, only for six measures!"

After another section of wild struggle, however, they realize that the "only possible alternative to this debacle is what was hinted at for the six measures previously. Eventually both instruments return to that and extend it to form a coda to the entire work. This time the melody is harmonized by a twelve-note chord with lots of tonal elements in it, pointing the way to a possible future stylistic synthesis, or at least common ground between styles."

Despite Ishmael's calculated approach to composition, his music had always been full of gorgeous melodies and interesting harmonies. Perhaps they had always distracted me so much that I had never quite realized how crucial to the music his structures were. But with the cello sonata, something happened. As I sat there listening, the music spoke to me more evocatively than words ever could have about his despair at the violence in the world and his hope for a future where people could live and work together. Just how organized musical pitches could have expressed all of that I still don't know, and yet as I listened I knew, without a doubt, that for Ishmael, music *is* language.

So did I now have it all straight? Just barely. Then it was time to move on, because already the kids' landscape was changing. Just as I was formulating my ideas about how they were learning music, they switched gears!

Imagine Vita now. She is sitting at the piano practicing "The Serenade of the Doll" from Debussy's *Children's Corner Suite*. She plays the opening section in different rhythms several times, first with the soft pedal and then without. Both Vita and Ishmael feel that using the soft pedal is somehow cheating — that they *should* be able to play as softly as they need to by developing the necessary control in their fingers and by concentrating totally on the sound that they want. I disagree. But then, I'm not the one trying to play the opening to the "Serenade."

Next, Vita practices the first theme in rhythms. Suddenly, she stops. "I never noticed this before! Look, when the theme comes back the second time it's not just that the notes are up a fifth, but that the fourth note goes down a fifth instead of up a fourth as you would expect. And when it comes back again, on the second page, it is up a whole octave from the first time, but once again the fourth note goes down a fifth. I'll have to show this to Ishmael!"

Could it be that Vita the musician/artist has now decided to become analytical? Just when I am sure that I have unravelled yet another mystery about how she and Ishmael learn and interpret the world (and have written it down), everything changes. Even Ishmael, once the "pure" musician, is now turning to art for inspiration.

"I just finished writing a cycle of four songs," he wrote to a friend the other day, "two in Italian, one in Spanish, and one in Portuguese, by twentieth-century poets. With the last I was very much helped by thinking of it in connection with a painting I saw long ago in the Museum of Modern Art. I have perhaps totally mythologized it by now, but the way I remember it is quite striking. I looked at it for a long time, and most of that time I felt as though I couldn't see anything — just a kind of disturbing reddish and whitish blur. Even as that it was very evocative. But eventually I realized it was a huge number of little distorted corpses! It's hard to say how the picture influenced the song, but I think that it helped me to write a very coloristic piece, in line with the violent color imagery of the poem."

In his autobiography, *Unfinished Journey*, Yehudi Menuhin describes his father sitting with him every day, "reading newspapers" while he practiced. Obviously, Mr. Menuhin figured he had nothing to teach Yehudi about how to practice or play the violin, I used to think. But did he imagine, then, that Yehudi wouldn't practice at all if he didn't sit there? I wondered. Now, years after reading the book, I know out of my own experience with Vita and Ishmael that there was no better way for Mr. Menuhin to keep in touch with Yehudi as Yehudi's ideas about music developed and changed. When Mr. Menuhin listened to Yehudi practice the Mendelssohn concerto, even if he could offer no technical help, he was learning the piece himself, learning the way Yehudi learned it and conceived of it. And surely Mr. Menuhin discovered with Yehudi, as I have with Vita and Ishmael, that by learning as much as he could about how Yehudi conceived of and worked on pieces, he enabled Yehudi to use him as a listener, to reflect back his own learning process in order to better understand how to give shape to his learning work.

When Vita and Ishmael begin learning a new piece, they tend to hear it from inside — not as a listener actually hears them playing it, but as the ideal sound they are striving for. As I listen to them play and watch how they work, I begin to hear the piece from inside, too; I begin to sense what it is they are hearing. At the same time, I remain the outside listener, the audience. Often, simply by being there as the listener, I help them bridge the gap between the sounds they hope to make and the sounds they sense I am hearing.

Sometimes, though, that isn't enough. Sometimes, as with Justin's composing, only time will help Vita and Ishmael to discover how to bring out the sounds and musical ideas they are striving for. Yet, just as Vita could not simply back away from Justin, I cannot simply back away from Vita and Ishmael. I have to let them know that I am still with them, ready to respond in any capacity that might be useful. Aside from patience, the greatest and most difficult lesson that this has forced me to learn is that in order to be able to keep their trust and respond to their work — and not just their music work — I have to be both willing to learn from them and able to change with them. I have to appreciate their fluidity and their differences of approach, and never insist on automatic coherence and method.

The Art of Copying

To Johann Sebastian Bach, Vivaldi was a revelation: Bach studied his works by copying and rearranging a number of Vivaldi's concertos until he felt secure in the "modern" Italian style. Bach's own concertos are indebted to Vivaldi, though Bach infused the facile Italian style with a goodly dose of German counterpoint.

— from *Great Masters of the Violin* by Boris Schwartz

Occasionally, Vita and Ishmael *do* invent for themselves clear-cut methods of working and leave no doubt as to what those methods are. But even when I can see that these methods work, I am also aware that they fly in the face of everything that schools allow or approve of.

"Always do your own work. Never copy other people's." This lesson haunts most of us throughout our school years. It is one that, until Vita and Ishmael managed to teach me otherwise, I accepted without question. Yet now it seems to be one of the major misconceptions about learning that the schools perpetrate.

When I was in first grade I shared a desk with a Mexican boy named Leonardo. His parents were migrant workers and for the first several months of school, I don't think he could speak a word of English. Was the teacher aware of this, or did she simply assume he was shy? Who knows? But in any case, because kids always find ways to communicate regardless of language barriers, all that I was really aware of was that he didn't know his "colors." Magnanimously, I used to show him the "correct" crayon to use, being sophisticated enough, or so I thought, to know that you should always color apples red and outline them in black.

When Leonardo copied my papers, which I let him do as a matter of course, he wrote my name, just as I did, in the space marked "NAME." I don't know about Leonardo, but it wasn't long before this communal approach to schoolwork got *me* into trouble.

My best friend, who was working well ahead of the rest of the class in math, suggested that I catch up with her by copying all of her answers into my math workbook. She knew that she was going to skip a grade and she wanted me to skip with her. Well, I didn't skip. I got caught copying instead. The teacher called me up to her desk and asked me how I had suddenly learned long division and double-digit multiplication. "I didn't," I admitted, feeling the kind of unspeakable shame and humiliation that we all eventually grow immune to in school. And yet I also remember that one afternoon, as I was busy filling in my workbook with my friend's answers, I had a sudden breakthrough about multiplication. "So *that's* what 'times' means! One number added up *as many times as* the other number. And it works both ways!" I spent the next morning at the bus stop cementing my discovery, excitedly solving the problems on the older children's flash cards. But how could I have explained my discovery to the teacher? I doubt I was even consciously aware of it.

In fifth or sixth grade, now considerably more sophisticated, I remember sitting at a long wooden table in a corner of the school library, trying to write a report about glaciers, a subject that I had hoped would be interesting but that now seemed far less so than the shelves of books tempting me from across the table. A *World Book Encyclopedia* lay closed by my elbow. I had made myself read the pertinent article several times over, but now I knew that I would really have to buckle down and write something. My mind was a total blank, though, which was irritating, and the thought of the closed encyclopedia was even more irritating. If only I could let myself open it again to borrow just a few key phrases. "Surely then I could get going," I thought longingly to myself.

Instead, I turned away from it as if from an enemy. It had given me all of the information I supposedly needed, but now it was exacting its price: by explaining everything so perfectly (in the best possible words, of course), it couldn't help but make me feel the inadequacy of my own words. Once again, as in first grade, not to mention time and time again throughout the intervening years, I felt humiliated.

Although they have always loved hearing stories about my childhood, I have never told these two stories to Vita and Ishmael. At twelve and fifteen, it hasn't yet occurred to them that copying someone else's work might be "bad," and I would never want to be the one to plant that seed in their minds. The real irony, though, is that when Ishmael first began his blatant copy work — when he first began copying out picture books word for word and then calling the writing his own — it didn't bother me, but only because at that time I had placed the responsibility for his academic training squarely in the hands of the schools. Since he wasn't yet of school age, I simply looked at what he did as "extra-curricular," fun and games.

In *Mindstorms*, Seymour Papert writes:

> After five years at Piaget's Center for Genetic Epistemology in Geneva, I came away impressed by his way of looking at children as the active builders of their own intellectual structures. But to say that intellectual structures are built by the learner rather than taught by a

teacher does not mean that they are built from nothing. On the contrary: Like other builders, children appropriate to their own use materials that they find about them....

When I sat struggling with the encyclopedia, I was trying to build from nothing, and that is exactly what my teachers encouraged. But Vita and Ishmael know better, in the same way that the young Bach, "whose own concertos are indebted to Vivaldi," knew better. It is precisely because originality has never been an issue for them that they have, by making free use of the materials at hand, been able to go about "building their own intellectual structures."

Vita said the other day, "Remember that *Night Before Christmas* book we used to have with the pop-up pictures on every page? I used to spend hours looking at it, even when it wasn't Christmas time. I really liked the idea of all those little pictures popping up, like the reindeer and the sugar plums, because they seemed so real — you know, three-dimensional. In fact, the first pop-up I ever made myself was a copy of one that was in that book. It was a house. Later, I copied a Santa for Mrs. Butler for a Christmas present."

And Ishmael, equally unselfconsciously, said recently as he explained to me how he began writing his cello sonata, "At first I wrote it without any conception of how to judge the chords, except by their not being tonal. That was just because of the structural reason that I wanted to include an atonal section. But it was pretty depressing writing that and then reading Steven Stucky's book on Lutoslawski's music, because Lutoslawski has a well-thought-out atonal harmony that he can rationally judge. In other words, the notes aren't arbitrary in the least. So I got very excited about that method of thinking about large atonal harmonies and I started using it for my own work."

Blatantly ignoring the example of artists, for example, who routinely sit in museums copying the works of the great masters, my teachers said, over and over again while I was in school, "Be sure to use your own words." Perhaps that is why when I memorized Wordsworth's famous poem *Daffodils*, although I obviously felt the beauty of the words, I also felt threatened by them, just as I had by that encyclopedia lying closed by my elbow on the library table.

"I'll never be able to write like that!" I remember thinking, as I sat in a big oak tree in my back yard repeating the lines to myself: "I wandered lonely as a cloud/That floats on high o'er vales and hills,/ When all at once I saw a crowd,/A host of golden daffodils..." It's almost certainly true. Yet Vita and Ishmael may still come close, simply because they never shy away from really wonderful language. Instead, they feel free to use it in whatever ways make sense.

From the time that they were old enough to string three or four words together to make a sentence, they memorized whole sections from the supposedly "much-too-hard" books we read aloud to them. Bob and I felt a bit guilty, naturally, for being so impatient to read all the books that we had grown up with and loved, but Vita and Ishmael didn't seem to mind. Often, they had no idea what was going on, and yet they sang or chanted their favorite passages to themselves throughout the day, feeling the words roll off their tongues, I often thought, the way they felt the silk linings on their baby blankets as they went to sleep.

I still remember Ishmael walking in circles around the garden, wearing a pair of Bob's big rain boots (and not much else), whispering under his breath, "'Good morning, Eeyore,' said Pooh. 'Good morning, Pooh Bear,' said Eeyore gloomily. 'If it *is* a good morning,' he said. 'Which I doubt,' said he." And then repeating, all over again, "'Good morning, Eeyore,' said Pooh. 'Good morning, Pooh Bear,' said Eeyore gloomily...."

By carrying passages around in their heads all day long, Vita and Ishmael gradually digested them ("So *that's* why Eeyore felt so bad. It was his birthday!") and absorbed the vocabulary and sentence structure for their own use. Words like "doubt" and "gloomy" became a part of their earliest everyday language. Often, they objected grumpily, "If it *is* a...."

As I said earlier, when he was four (and could not yet read, by the way) Ishmael (and later Vita — she more artist than scribe, however) spent concentrated hours copying out picture books. He liked to staple his pages together when he was done to make "real" books — *his* books, as he always called them. A few years later, as I described in *Better Than School*, when Ishmael wrote a little essay on "How to Make a Book," his conception of the process *still* had nothing to do with originality — it was all purely technical, and apparently quite easy: "Start with twenty pieces of paper, then fold them and take a sheet of construction paper and fold it and open it up and put the folded paper inside it and sew it down the back — over, under, over, under. And write in it. And there is your book!"

Glenn Doman, author of *How to Teach Your Baby to Read*, writes that "if you teach a child the facts, he will intuit the rules." Vita, with her pop-ups, did just that, although to be honest, she taught herself "the facts" as well.

"Pretty soon I got tired of making pop-ups the way the book did," she told me, "because I started making cards and I wanted them to open up a different way. So I spent a while experimenting with making things that just stood up, not worrying at all about making them so that they'd fold up again when the card closed. Finally after I'd made a card with a tree that stood up properly, I just sort of forcibly closed it, not caring about how the tree got creased or folded up or anything. When I opened it up again, the tree stood up exactly the way I wanted it to. It had worked!"

And Ishmael with his cello sonata? Well, as his composition teacher tried to explain to me, "It's true that Ishmael is drawing his ideas from Lutoslawski, but in the process he is developing a whole new musical language of his own."

As with Vita's pop-ups and Ishmael's composition work, by disregarding all notions of originality — by memorizing and copying other people's words — Vita and Ishmael were, in effect, collecting the facts they needed to be able to grasp, intuitively, the rules of general language usage. By building, so to speak, on other people's words, phrases, punctuation, and sentence structures, they taught themselves how to shape their letters, spell, punctuate, and eventually, how to write smoothly flowing prose. They were teaching themselves to read in the process of "writing books" when they mouthed the words they held in their minds as they copied them down.

In schools, where, as in so many other areas of life, we have forsaken intuition in favor of professionalism, the approach teachers most often take is completely opposite to the model that children develop for themselves in their early learning. Fortunately, Ishmael and Vita were able, for the most part, to learn to read and write the way they learned to speak. Ishmael, because he learned before he ever went to school, and Vita because she never went to school at all, were able to hold back, to wait, until they had gained enough practical knowledge of the way language worked — enough practical experience with language through copy work, among other things — to be able to intuit and come to terms with the rules of phonics simply as "laws of nature."

In a letter that later formed the basis for his article about homeschooling in the *Journal of Orgonomy*, my friend John Lampkin wrote, "In schools, the abstract intellect reigns supreme... and the rules of word formation and phonics are taught first. Abstraction and reasoning, instead of being a natural outgrowth of factual knowledge, become displaced." Although we generally think of school educators as the inventors of rote learning, and schools as places that expect children to acquire factual knowledge at the expense of their own independent thinking, abstractions, as John Lampkin points out, are what schools expect children to memorize: rules, skills, and facts that have nothing to do with real children's lives.

"We teach children about suffixes and prefixes," a teacher once explained to me, "to increase their vocabularies," as if it had never occurred to her that children would more easily increase their vocabularies by learning new words that had real significance to their lives — words they came across in their own reading or heard while talking with other people.

And as Ishmael's teacher wrote in a report to the assistant superintendent, "Ishmael seems more comfortable at a third grade reading level; he still makes some mistakes in phonics and vocabulary skills. Testing should be continued before considering a higher level. The testing should only be for reading skills, as I already know that he can read adult materials."

John Holt, who knew the dangers inherent in deciding that we have to teach children certain skills, fantasized about something similar in *How Children Learn:*

> Suppose we decided that we had to "teach" children to speak. How would we go about it? First, some committee of experts would analyze speech and break it down into a number of separate "speech skills." We would probably say that, since speech is made up of sounds, a child must be taught to make all the sounds of his language before he can be taught to speak the language itself. Doubtless we would list these sounds, easiest and commonest ones first, harder and rarer ones next. Then we would begin to teach infants these sounds, working our way down the list.... Everything would be planned, with nothing left to chance; there would be plenty of drill, review and tests, to make sure that he had not forgotten anything."

What a disaster it would be if young children had to learn to speak in school! Still, it's pretty amazing just to think of the hundreds of words that they all learn without ever asking us the meaning or running to consult a dictionary. They listen for meanings within whole contexts and, not afraid of exposing their own ignorance, they guess and experiment aloud, using strange words in their own speech as if by accident.

I think of a young friend, Amanda Bergson-Shilcock, who when she was ten wrote, in response to the commonly asked question, "Do you ever go anyplace outside your home?" that she included in a question-and-answer sheet about homeschooling for her state legislature, "That has something to do with the question 'Do you consider yourself a social outcast?' but it also *evokes* a different answer [my emphasis]."

No dictionary could have told Amanda how to use the word "evoke" more accurately. A teacher (or her mother), by suggesting that she use a more appropriate word, might have scared her away from ever using it again. Yet left on her own to experiment with the word in different contexts, she will gradually discern its precise conventional usage.

The other day, Vita, when talking about how strange it is that "rough" and "dough" are spelled alike but sound so different, suddenly thought of the word "sough." "How is that pronounced?" she asked, meanwhile pronouncing it like "rough."

"Is it even a word?" I said. "I've never heard of it."

"Well," Vita said, "Rain soughs. I read someplace that 'the rain soughed outside.'"

I looked up the word and sure enough, there it was (pronounced both suf and sou). The dictionary, of course, gave a more specific definition than Vita was able to — "a soft murmuring or rustling sound" — and yet despite the fact that Vita couldn't actually tell me what "sough" meant, it was already part of her active vocabulary. By trusting herself she had been able to intuit an accurate usage within an appropriate context. Now, by using the word often enough and by hearing other people use it — "by using her reservoir of factual knowledge as a base," as John Lampkin put it — she will gradually be able to extract a precise definition.

Vita and Ishmael, when they began to read, gradually increased their reading vocabularies through this same process. By reading within whole contexts, they guessed at strange words in order to make sense of phrases and sentences. I know a nine-year-old girl who can read books like *Stuart Little* fluently, but still can't read random lists of words out of context with any degree of accuracy. (Hence, the school considers her unable to read because she does so poorly on their reading placement test, which is exactly that: random lists of words.) But in time, as she reads real books with real meanings, even she will internalize most, if not all, of the phonetic rules and their exceptions, simply through a process of trial and error.

Yet schools, when they teach reading and writing as if they were a series of disjointed skills to be learned progressively, teach children to mistrust their own intuition, by ignoring and, in the case of Ishmael, even discouraging the child's highly experimental learning process. And by replacing that natural process with carefully laid out and systematic "rules" and exceptions that children must memorize, the schools teach them to be suspicious of their own guesswork and terrified of their own ignorance.

Ishmael felt thoroughly traumatized in school when (despite the fact that he could read) he couldn't immediately distinguish "long" and "short" vowel sounds or recognize consonant blends. He was traumatized when he couldn't alphabetize long lists of words (although he could already use a dictionary), and handwriting was constant torture for him because he was so afraid of shaping his letters the "wrong" way.

Children who, as John Holt put it, "observe, wonder, find, or make and then test the answers to the questions they ask themselves" have no conscious sense of "wrong" because like scientists, they are involved in a continual process of moving closer towards what is right — of defining and redefining their views of the world.

Vita, never imagining that there might be one right way, taught herself how to write her own letters, sometimes with pastels or paints, but never limiting herself to pens and pencils, while she sat at the kitchen table with Ishmael each morning as he did his schoolwork.

At first, it was a chore for her to shape each letter. It was like free drawing, since we gave her no system to work from, and her goal was simply to match, as best she could, the shapes of the letters that she copied. Later, she experimented with intricate and highly ornamented letters, and finally, when she wanted to write whole words, speed became important. She learned, through months of unconscious experimentation, to find ways of shaping her letters using as few pencil strokes and lifts as possible. By the time she was six or seven, with few exceptions and no trauma whatsoever, she had learned to form her letters just the way Ishmael did (or you and I do, for that matter).

In school I learned to be afraid of what I didn't know and yet I learned not to ask questions, not only because I was afraid to expose my own ignorance but because I stopped expecting to understand the answers. That is exactly what happened to Ishmael when I tried to teach him how to read, using an easy-to-read book called *Little Bear*. As I wrote in *Better Than School*:

> The first word was "What" — an awful word, really. I later learned that in school it is called a "key word" — a word you just have to memorize, with no apologies given. But I apologized to Ishmael. It was embarrassing to have to try to explain just why the word "what" didn't sound like "waahat." "Will" went a little better, and I hastily told Ishmael to forget about the silent "e" in "little" since I didn't know what it was doing there. "Bear" didn't make any sense, but once he accepted that b-e-a-r really did spell "bear," he managed to read "wear" on his own.

If Ishmael was merely exhausted at the end of that session, I was semi-hysterical. "This isn't my job anyway," I assured myself. "After all, I've got to leave something for his first grade teacher to do." I may have been right to think, at the time, that Ishmael had been on the verge of reading, yet in my impatience all that I accomplished by trying to speed up the process was to teach him how much he didn't know and to convince him that the whole language was incomprehensible, at least in terms of the logical phonetic system I was trying to explain to him.

Over time, Ishmael must have recovered from that disastrous reading session and, later, from his year and a half of schooling. Now, like Vita, he seldom seems overwhelmed by the enormity of what he doesn't know. Like three-year-olds who constantly ask "Why? Why?" he and Vita are still blissfully sure, as they ought to be, of finding answers to their questions. And never feeling ashamed of what they don't know, they ask questions mercilessly! When I'm not in the hot seat, the scene can be pretty funny.

The other day, Bob and the kids sat on the porch reading from D'Arcy Thompson's *On Growth and Form*. It is a difficult book — philosophical, scientific, and mathematical. Sentence by sentence, almost, Vita and Ishmael stopped Bob, literally demanding explanations. But often, although he had studied the book carefully, he had no ready answers. He squirmed (just a little bit!) and the kids were rightfully indignant at his apparent laziness. In the same way that I can sit over lunch with Ishmael while he tells me about his latest musical discovery and not ask him what he's talking about, for God's sake, it was plain (even to the kids) that Bob, too, is apt to slide over what he doesn't understand, not as part of the ongoing process involved in jumping right into something difficult out of interest and curiosity, as Vita and Ishmael do, but out of unconscious adult fear and disinterest.

Vita and Ishmael ask questions, confident of finding answers, and yet, contradictory as this may seem, they are at the same time perfectly comfortable living with the ambiguity of what they *don't* understand. Vita said the other day, "You know, I've read *Little Women* at least ten times, but for the first few times I didn't even know what was going on. I just liked the book and so I kept reading it." She said that so casually and happily that I realized that she felt *no* guilt, as if she had no notion at all that she "should" understand everything she reads (just as baby Ishmael had had no notion that he should understand *Winnie-the-Pooh*).

How different from the attitude I learned in school. There, I was taught from day one to "read for comprehension." Reading a book over again implied failure. When we came to a word we didn't know we felt guilty if we didn't look it up in our *Webster's Junior Dictionary*. We inched along from reading level to reading level, always threatened by the lists of questions and vocabulary words at the end of each chapter. Even in Ishmael's first grade class, where you'd think the teacher would have been overjoyed by his eagerness to read, she punished him for reading ahead in his reader. "You mustn't look ahead," she told him, "until I've had a chance to make certain that you understand the story I've just assigned you."

"I've just been reading *The Mill on the Floss*," Vita said to me, "and I can barely put it down."

"Yes, I've noticed," I answered, smiling, thinking of all the other work she hadn't done.

"But the thing is," Vita persisted, "just when the story seems to be moving along, George Eliot starts moralizing, as if she's just sitting there writing thoughts as they occur to her. I skip those parts."

"Oh, Vita," I thought, "but those are my very favorite parts!" Yet I wasn't unhappy. Certainly I didn't think that she should go back, read them, and try to comprehend them. I knew from experience, now, that someday — next week, perhaps next month, or next year — Vita *would* read those passages, and that eventually, she might learn to love them the way I do. But for now, the great thing is that she doesn't feel threatened by them — by what is still too difficult for her

— just as, when she was first learning how to read, she didn't feel threatened by all the words that she didn't yet know.

Just recently, actually, she told me a fascinating story about one of those words: "I remember reading one of Ishmael's 'Tom and Mickey' stories," she said, "about how they escaped to an island, and I kept wondering what an *is*-land was. I don't remember how I figured it out, except that Ishmael kept talking about the island that they were on and after a while I guess I just realized that the only word in the story that could possibly be island was *is* -land."

Strange as it seems, Ishmael wrote that story when Vita was no more than four-and-a-half or five, *a year or more* before she or any of us would have said that she could read. Yet she remembers pondering one of the more blatant perversities of the English language without any seeming anxiety.

John Holt wrote in *How Children Learn* about children learning how to read:

> They have a lot of very tentative hunches about connections between the look of printed letters and the sounds of spoken words.... But if we put too much pressure on those hunches, by continually asking children questions about what this or that letter says, we are liable to jar those hunches loose altogether and convince the children that they don't know anything, can't figure out anything, and must depend on us for all of their information.

When we take it for granted that there is a clear distinction between knowing and not knowing ("Vita can't yet read"), we tend to become so sure of "right" answers that we don't realize the importance of allowing children to discover for themselves what is right, and to develop their own solutions and their own methods for arriving at those solutions. Out of impatience with our children's tentativeness, as John puts it, and a suspicion of their chosen methods, we all too often threaten their ability as scientists and separate them from their own curiosity. Once humiliated by my second grade teacher, I lost all sense of the meaning of multiplication. It took me years to rediscover it.

Reading
and Writing

Creativity... is the retention throughout life of something that belongs properly to the infant experience: the ability to create the world.

— D.W. Winnicott in *Home is Where We Start From: Essays in Psychoanalysis*

If children build the rudiments of their early language — speech, reading, grammar, and spelling — unconsciously, through guess-work and constant experimentation, using imitation as their first building block, it is precisely this process, too, that is the key to their development as writers, since writing is simply an extension of speech.

Vita and Ishmael, the constant experimenters, taught themselves to write the same way they taught themselves to speak and to read — by using the real world as their teacher and defining and redefining their relationship to it as they learned how to use it to pursue their work. Often, they worked on reading and writing simultaneously. But while reading and writing, for them, developed out of the same process, my responses to their reading and writing ended up being quite different. I was at once far more involved with their writing than with their reading and equally distant — more involved in my role as a writer, equally distant in my role as a teacher. Perhaps this is because once we learn how to read — once we have that first breakthrough about how the black squiggles on a page represent sounds, words, and meaning — our learning process becomes a private and self-reinforcing one, involving, more than anything, simply reading more. Writing, on the other hand, because it is essentially a social tool that, to have any meaning at all, demands a relationship between two or more people (or two or more sides of ourselves), also demands the active response of other people as we try to make our written communication more accessible and our words a truer representation of our original intent. Unfortunately, we too often think of writing in terms of basic writing skills, such as letter formation and spelling. Yet as with reading skills, those basic writing skills have very little to do with real writing (whether that writing is a utilitarian or creative endeavor). Beyond simply learning to write, then, we are forever learning to become writers. There can be no end to the process, or to our need for other people, other readers.

Ishmael, as I have said, was a born speller. He never drew pictures, he drew letters. He graduated from copy work to writing original short stories even before he went to first grade. If we see writing simply as a form of communication, then my involvement with Ishmael's early writing was almost entirely as a receiver of communication — as a reader.

Vita was neither a speller nor always a determined communicator. One of the magnificent (and often frustrating) things about her is just how free she is from the confines that school values manage to place on most of us. When she was little we used to call her fierce. What a temper! Sometimes I'd watch her sitting at the kitchen table drawing with her pens, and the only image that came to mind was the darkness of an impending storm, the anticipation of tumult and violence. When, or at what, would she fly out next? Needless to say, she was what the schools would have considered thoroughly undisciplined. She couldn't imagine narrowing her learning about the world down to "the skills the school people think I ought to know." She couldn't have helped but know, even then, something of what those skills might be, but I think it seemed absurd to her to imagine that *only* those skills would be important enough to spend the best part of a day working at.

It would have been far easier in terms of our dealings with the school district if Vita had learned to write and spell and even add in the conventional way, but, well, there was always her temper to contend with, and when she wanted to draw, she wanted to draw. Now, she wanted to do what Ishmael did, too. She wanted to read and write and do math, but once again, in her own way. Often, her way meant making a picture out of every letter she wrote, reading the words she thought the author ought to have written, or deciding on answers to math problems that to her alone made sense.

Speech is both melodic and rhythmic, and writing, like speech, can only convey meaning (or purpose, as was sometimes a better way to describe Vita's reason for picking up a pen) when it too follows the melodic and rhythmic lines of the language. Vita, like Ishmael, never for a moment doubted this. She listened to the flow of the talk around her (and the language in the books we read aloud to her), and regardless of the sense she made, she always managed to capture on paper the melodic essence of the language she heard around her.

Nobody ever told Vita about the rules for writing correctly — about the need for a subject and predicate in every complete sentence, or about the parts of speech, or the rules of punctuation. Because of this she never learned to think of writing as a string of disassociated grammatical skills divorced from speech, the way the children in Ishmael's first grade class surely must have. Our neglect, if you will, was the result of chance, timing, and our response to Vita's temperament, and yet I now see that if I had ever really decided to sit down and help Vita with the mechanics of writing, I would have made writing all the harder for her, since I would have put the mechanics between her ear for language and what she wanted to say, or at least accomplish.

Babies "learn to speak by speaking," John Holt wrote in *Instead of Education*. "The baby who begins to talk, long before he makes any sounds that we hear as words, has learned from sharp observation that the sounds that bigger people make with their mouths affect other things that they do. *Their talk makes things happen.*"

Even in their early writing, Vita and Ishmael used grammar and punctuation to create the rhythms, and hence the meanings, that they wanted in order to make things happen. They felt absolute confidence in their ability, like the babies John described, and yet correctness, as such, was simply not an issue for them. With Ishmael, it had come too easily to think or worry about; with Vita, it was irrelevant to her initial intentions.

At first, for example, she didn't use periods to end sentences or capitals to begin them because she didn't like the idea of creating full stops on paper. Language, to her, wasn't that choppy, and although she knew, from reading aloud, that her breath would force necessary pauses, she didn't yet trust her readers to understand the subtle intentions of a period. In fact, when I read her writing aloud, it usually came out just right:

> I am going To be in The "Sicrit gardin" I know haLf of IT already I am a pansy in The Sicrit gardin' acshooaly iT is called "Mandy's seecrit Gardin"

Gradually, though, Vita saw the risk of not punctuating, or of using commas, for example, rather than periods to create sentence endings. She often found that she wanted her readers to pause longer than they did when they saw only a comma or no punctuation mark at all. When communication *was* one of her immediate goals, it became increasingly frustrating to her when she saw what a difficult time they had plowing through her prose. Because she never thought of punctuation in terms of a skill or a set of rules, though, she was determined to keep on experimenting until she arrived at what she considered to be the best way to convey on paper the precise rhythmic flow she intended.

Ishmael, by the way, does the same thing when he experiments with meters and note lengths in the pieces he composes. Composition, in fact, has never been bound by rules the way spelling and writing have, thanks to Samuel Johnson, Webster, and later eager grammarians. Perhaps because the language of music is still changing so rapidly, its grammar has been left wide open to accomodate the change. Composers take it for granted that they must, in a sense, create a new grammar for every piece they write. It is simply part of the process. In any case, far more than Ishmael, who had always seen the rules of language usage as a given, Vita experimented, at first with stops — with colons, semi-colons, dashes, and commas — to see how her readers responded and to discover for herself how she could best control their response.

Vita didn't see the rules of spelling as givens, either. One spelling seemed as arbitrary as the next to her, one more aesthetically pleasing one day, another more aesthetically pleasing the next. Sometimes, communicating on paper, even when she was writing, was simply not on Vita's agenda. Sometimes she saw writing as art more than anything else. From the moment Ishmael brought one home and opened it, Vita was fascinated by spellers, for example. By the time she could shape her letters, she could work through a chapter of a workbook in no time and get a perfect score on the spelling test at the end. But then she went back to spelling her own way. It was as if the fact that there is one correct way to spell a word had no relevance for her as long as creating art was her main reason for writing. More than anything, she used the spellers as just another excuse to do art — spellers were a pleasant change from blank white paper. She marked them up with fancy colored pens, experimented with various styles of handwriting, and a bit like Andy Warhol with his soup cans, thought in terms of artistic caricature. A perfect score in a workbook, the answers pencilled in perfect grade-school printing, no less, seemed creatively satisfying to her.

To be fair to Vita, though, I should say that at the same time she used writing to make art (or simply to experiment with sound and pacing), she also wrote real notes and stories and made "books," much the way Ishmael had a few years earlier. Writers were everywhere in her life, and despite her troubles with punctuation and spelling, I don't think she ever questioned the communication functions that writing could serve. It's just that in a spirit of independence, she added new functions of her own!

When storytelling (not art) was on her mind, it was most important to Vita, at least at first, to convey her messages quickly and easily (i.e., without a moment's thought as to what might or might not be correct). Producing a sentence like "'Giv me a hand dear' said the whte haird lade as she cmpledid a strach split," served her purpose perfectly. She saw no reason to improve on it.

Later, though, she grew tired of having to translate everything she wrote for her readers. It was no longer fun to hand her grandmother a story about ballet if her grandmother wasn't even going to attempt to read it on her own. "'Those ballat dams wir pirfikly happy being vrtacl for a coupl of handrid yrs,'" her white-haired lady continued, much to my amusement, "'and I had to invant dantsing that lis, rols, luxurats on the flor.'"

"Very nice, Vita," her grandmother might say. "Could you read it to me?"

Vita would have liked to write like "big people," as John Holt called them, but her difficulty was that she still refused to accept without a doubt that there was only one way to spell a word. She thought of correct spelling as spelling that we adults approved of rather than as spelling that was objectively correct. When spelling to please or accommodate adults was important to her, then, her solution was to ask for help with every word, even the words we knew she could spell herself. Of course, her dependence on us grew as tiring and as frustrating to her as her grandmother's lack of comprehension, and so, perhaps as a kind of respite, she often went back, for days at a time, to the slap-dash notes and stories that only we could read.

Like her white-haired lady who invented dancing that rolled and luxuriated, Vita had, for whatever reason, to explore the realms of written language and discover spelling, like punctuation, for herself. I was anything but complacent during the process, since I had no idea what the end result would be. Yet I felt that my hands were tied, because every time I stepped in and tried to interfere (or, to do myself justice, tried to help), Vita simply stopped writing. Out of love for her stories and her calligraphy I quickly learned to keep my distance.

For most children, the process that real writers go through in order to write stories, essays, and books is a complete mystery. They not only have no idea how books are made, physically, but they know nothing about the function of editors, copy-editors, and proofreaders. Even more important, they can't imagine our struggles; the threat or joy that we feel as we sit down to a blank page; the way the writing can simply flow or suddenly stop; the whole process of revising, rewriting, and throwing endless crumpled balls of paper into the waste basket. Vita and Ishmael saw it all — there were no secrets. And beyond that, they saw the way Bob and I used each other as critics. They saw my relief when Bob said, "You know, the sentence would probably work better this way," and my fear that he might simply be giving up on me when he said, "It's fine." Vita and Ishmael quickly learned that writing is almost never fine — that there's usually something you can do to make it better.

As writers, then, Vita and Ishmael used us the way Bob and I used each other, as colleagues rather than simply as teachers. Vita didn't want unasked-for help with spelling, but she certainly wanted help with style and clarity, even at four or five. When I wrote to my friend Manfred Smith about my work with Vita and Ishmael, he wrote back, "I recall essays returned by teachers who had obviously attempted suicide while grading my papers: red ink everywhere! I shudder to think of myself as the poor student, but I suppose it's all a matter of relationship...."

I'm still not sure what Manfred meant by "relationship," but giving him the benefit of the doubt, I would say he's absolutely right: it's all a matter of the relationship of a writer to his or her own writing. That is, in school, a teacher's red ink becomes her claim to the writing, but as Vita and Ishmael saw every day at home, red ink (or more politely, red pencil) could mean just the opposite. Vita and Ishmael always delighted in the process of working with us as writers because it helped them to see and lay claim to their writing in new ways. And for Vita, it represented a process, a kind of exploration, that simply following solid rules of grammar did not.

By the time she was ten, Vita had learned to spell — or rather, had decided to use standard spelling — although both she and I still rely a lot on Ishmael and on our good old *Webster's*. But although she has opted for correctness, she has never abandoned her preoccupation with process — with the development of language usage. She still writes and rewrites sentences and tears sheets out of the typewriter and crumples them up, the way I do, and she, like Ishmael, still comes to ask me to help her rework a phrase or line. That is not surprising to me. What has taken me by total surprise, though, is her fascination with the way other people use — or, more precisely, misuse or make free with — language. She jumps with glee at the added apostrophes on signs she sees in town ("Church's Carpet's" or "Typewriter's Repaired") and with the free use of quotation marks she discovers on restaurant menus ("hot" soup or "fresh" fish). And if she now spells correctly and writes flowing, melodic prose, her current alter ego Vite (so-named after the inspiring examples of "nite," "lite," and "rite") writes to a totally different beat. In a letter to a mutual friend, for example, Vite wrote the news about Vita's latest bakery venture:

> You know, we kinda decided to move VITA'S BAKE SHOP to the new co-op that opened in Collegetown? And a... we, like, thought we'd (kinda) change the name to make it, like, well you know, more, like, student-oriented? So we kinda thought, like we could call it something like, you know, E. Norma's Cookies or something?... 'Cause when we went to Philly last time, we kinda got, like, inspired, 'cause we saw these two places in Scranton, and, like, man, they were called Econolodge and um ContempriInn, and we just thought, like, Monster!

Vita is interested in the problems of modern-day language usage and how people solve them. Vite takes a back-handed interest. After listening in on a conversation I had over lunch with an editor at a university press, Vita turned to Vite for help in an attempt to arrive at the perfect non-sexist style, following guidelines the editor said were considered to be acceptable. Vite, I'm afraid, offered more input than was perhaps advisable:

> 1. In most cases, the employee is given plenty of time to eat his lunch. However in some instances, she is under so much pressure that he doesn't get any time to eat her lunch at all. In still other cases there is so little time that he gets indigestion.
> 2. Everybody eats their lunch. Someone is eating their sandwich neatly.
> 3. S/he is eating h/er/is sandwich with ketchup.

Vite has discovered, in a dramatic way, that writing isn't just a functional skill; it can take on a whole aesthetic of its own, even as it draws from the music of speech. Vita and Ishmael know this, too. Even when they were three and four, and first copying out the words of A.A. Milne and Kenneth Grahame, they were becoming aware that great writers (like great composers) work in their own distinct and recognizable styles. Their ears picked up and their writing hands could feel the differences between Milne and Grahame the way they would later pick up and feel the unique characteristics of Bach, Mozart, and Beethoven.

When Ishmael was ten he learned his first Beethoven sonata. It was a real struggle. Yet when he learned his next Beethoven sonata, it came almost easily, as if his mind and fingers had intuitively begun to come to grips with the underlying structure (grammar) of Beethoven's language. The same was true when Vita learned a Mozart piano concerto. Clearly it had been the sonata that she had struggled with six months earlier that had begun to unlock for her the mysteries of Mozart. (Not that it's ever possible be unlock *all* the mysteries of a Mozart or a Beethoven, but that's their enduring fascination.)

As I described in *Better Than School,* Ishmael had no concern for originality when he moved from copying stories to actually writing his own. He had already absorbed not only the underlying structures and music of everyday speech but the grammatical structures of the writers he had come to love, and he borrowed freely from them in his own work. He had characters and plots that he wanted to bring to life, but they seemed to live in his imagination and on paper only within the flow of a specific aesthetic. Inspiration from Stevenson's *Kidnapped* lasted him for years. "The priest came around the corner," Ishmael wrote when he was eight or nine. "He was carrying my bag. He quickly told me not to start believing in any of the heresies, gave me a recipe for lily-of-the-valley wine, and bid me fervently good-bye." Another story from the same period was shaped by *Oliver Twist*: "His friends crowded about him, from old alleys where they had been stoning cats, from mansions in which they had been exploring, and all of them were ragged."

Most often, as Vita and Ishmael must have observed, the stylistic aesthetic in a piece of writing is determined not only by the specific writer, but by his or her chosen form. We write journals and letters in a totally different style from, say, mystery stories or advertisements or newspaper editorials. I remember John Holt on one of his visits to us, pacing the kitchen floor and saying with some agitation, "Some people just don't understand! Tennis would be no fun at all if we simply hit the ball whenever we liked. It's the court, the net, and even the rules of scoring that make the game worth playing at all."

As if inspired by the very limitations (net, court) that these forms establish, Vita and Ishmael have always experimented in their own writing with different literary styles, imitating (or more accurately, intuiting the rules of) the grammatical structures that the specific form demands.

Ishmael, who began by writing stories, went on, for several years, to work on journals, in response to a writer who advised him to "write what you know about." He experimented with writing simple factual outlines of each day, like the early diarists he'd read about ("October 7th, 1978, Saturday: I made a dugout. I went on a bike ride. I went hunting.") and sometimes, he did away with chronologies altogether, simply writing descriptively ("The sky is very bluish today; a huge, rather lopsided cloud is floating in the west. The sun is shining fiercely through scattered shreds of cloud in the east") or philosophically ("The good thing about coldness is that you can't be sluggish, even when you are freezing to death.").

In Vita's early writing, meanwhile, she mostly chose to imitate the forms and styles of her one and only "great master," Ishmael. Her stories, diaries, and neighborhood newspapers were all modeled on his. Yet with her letter writing, and from even before she could read, she has been involved in regular correspondences with adult friends. Her style developed through direct and unashamed imitations of theirs. To John Holt, who wrote:

> Walking through the Public Garden on this cool gray day, I saw something that I have never seen in the 26 years I have been in Boston — baby squirrels!
>
> We have jillions of squirrels in the Public Garden. People feed them, so they are very tame; a few years ago I stopped to watch a couple and one of them came right over *and ran up my pants leg and stuck his nose in my pocket!* But there wasn't any food there. Most aren't quite that bold, but they will eat out of your hand.
>
> But you never see them on the ground until they are pretty well grown. Today I saw some really young ones....

Vita replied:

> Looking out the window on this windy cold day, I saw something that I see every day (since we built a birdfeeder) — a squirrel!
>
> We have millions of squirrels here in Ithaca. We are the only people who feed them.
>
> About a month ago we saw about four to six pretty young ones, about half the size of the big ones....

And just as John ended his letter with:

Working away on Minuet II. One problem I have is that when things get complicated my third finger forgets which string it's on.

So Vita ended hers:

Working away on my second concerto. One problem I have is that when things get complicated my third finger forgets to play in tune.

And to her friend Benji Brown, who, she says, writes the most wonderful letters about nothing, she wrote:

I'm happy that spring really has come. At least I think it has. It snowed two days ago, after the most beautiful three days of sun and flowers, and today there was half an inch of snow on the ground and it was snowing! So why do I say spring has come, you ask? Because when I went outside after washing the dishes, it had all disappeared! (The snow I mean, not the outside!)

Unlike Ishmael, Vita (as well as Vite) has always been fascinated, both stylistically and graphically, with catalogues and brochures. Just as when I was little and sat at my work table, licking my finger and swooshing the pages of thick telephone books and dictionaries as I turned them, playing secretary (that dates me, right?), so Vita experiments with forms of commercial writing and syntax. "I've noticed that advertisement writers don't stay within the bounds of good grammar," Vita told me, a few years before Vite arrived on the scene in her full glory, "and I'm sure it's just a way for them to catch the attention of readers." Both in play, and yet with every intention of serious professionalism, she blends her love of language with that of art.

For instance, there is the tour guide she wrote for her science museum when she was eight:

For this summer, we have picked the elements (except for fire) as a main subject for the exhibits.
For earth, we have two exhibits:
Exhibit One is made up of nuts. We have Hickory, Eucalyptus, Black Walnut, and Butternut. We also included a Redwood cone. The

Hickory, Black Walnut and Butternut are closely related to each other, although Hickories make up a family of their own. Butternut Hickory, Pecan and Mockernut Hickory are all in the Hickory family, although we have only included the Shagbark Hickory in our collection. We are indebted to Nancy Wallace for bringing back the Eucalyptus nut for our collection.

...her descriptions of Christmas cards in her "Good Buys Catalogue" from last year:

A) Glittering gold notes adorn our handsome Musical Christmas card. Tree in center supports musical rainbow with notes. Please specify message.

B) Same as above but with added bonus: *Pop up Santa* pops up with a jolly laugh as you open the card. No message. (Santas vary)

...and even her annotations in her photo album of spring flowers:

Tulips abound at the Irving Place Conservatory. These are but a few of the many.

These structural and grammatical forms still inspire Vita's experimental use of language unconsciously, as other, usually more literary forms once inspired Ishmael. But now, at fifteen, Ishmael often experiments self-consciously, as in his "academic" writing, for example, when he wrote a paper called "Christianity and Mutual Aid":

In the concluding chapters of his novel *Anna Karenina* Tolstoy puts forth one of the simplest and (or so it appears at first glance) most difficult to argue with proofs of the existence of God that has ever been propounded. Surprisingly enough, however, as far as I know it has not received half as much attention as his ethical ideas. It is my intention in this essay to put it through some tests, with the object of finding out just how well it actually works.

...or in his paper about Rudolph Bahro's book, *The Alternative in Eastern Europe*.

The major things in the book that I wish to write about are
1) his extension of the Marxist model of historical development in order to form a theory of state — or, as he puts it, proto-socialism;

2) his immanent critique of proto-socialism; and
3) his program of "cultural revolution."

For Ishmael, though, it has been writing poetry, with all of its formalistic possibilities, that has captured his imagination the most. For years, he has pored over Clement Wood's three-inch-thick rhyming dictionary, practically memorizing the whole first two sections, "The Complete Formbook for Poets" and "The Fixed Form." He memorized the names of the metric feet, just as Clement Wood laid them out (Iamb, Trochee, Pyrrhic, etc.) and he even memorized Wood's examples of "flawless metric lines" ("Listen to this 3-foot amphimacer: 'Men of Rome, fight and die, never yield!'"). He memorized Wood's examples of "horrible" verse, delighting us at dinner with "'Ne'er did I see a ray of light/So strangely, lovely, warmly bright — /A stream of red as flashing by/'Gainst fair Aurora's azure sky....'" Now, with a sense of strict discipline, he writes his own sonnets, triolets, villanelles and haiku.

In the opera Ishmael is currently writing, about a prison uprising and life in the underworld, he is not only experimenting with international styles of music but also, in the libretto, with several distinct poetic forms. For example, there is Riyad's Ballad, "written in alternate 4 accent and 3 accent lines and rhymed 1,2,3,2":

Dolores, I should tell you — I
Am another man as well:
The famous hero Robin Hood,
Who formerly used to dwell
With his merry men in Sherwood Forest.
Their life was close to the earth,
And good as well, Dolores, for
They gave each man his worth:
They robbed the rich, but they gave to the poor
We needn't stand around
In slums, like you said — Let's rob and be merry,
And become like Robin, renowned.

And a traditional three-line blues:

My wings are clipped, and what's ahead of me?
My wings are clipped, and what's ahead of me?
Oh, nothing else but just more misery...

And, as Ishmael says, "a common sestet, written in iambic pen-
tameter, with the rhyme scheme 1,2,1,2,3,3":

> We'll hang him by his ankles over a well
> And station a mouse to nibble at the line,
> With a placard standing by to tell
> The moral to all who read: Don't be a swine.
> Don't tyrannize poor prisoners 'till they go
> And string you up to a death both cruel and slow.

In addition to being fascinated by specific forms of writing,
Ishmael also looks critically at the relationship of function to form in
other people's writing. He is an avid reader of program notes at
concerts, for example, yet often he finds them stylistically obscure
and unilluminating. "I have so often criticized the writers of program
notes for lapsing into musical jargon..." he wrote to a friend.

In his own program notes, although he is very careful to follow the
"rules" by including the usual historical, biographical, and analytical
detail and information, with a respectable amount of technical
language thrown in to provide the "necessary" academic weightiness,
the heart of his writing is really in reaction to all of that, as he struggles
to express his own ideas and discoveries about the pieces he is playing
as clearly as possible. "...[B]ut now," Ishmael admitted, as he continued on in his letter, "I find it very difficult to say things about pieces
that do not require using jargon."

For example, about Messiaen's *Canteyojaya*, he wrote:

> Before talking at length about Messiaen's style it should be pointed
> out that his music is very eclectic, in a certain way. One way to
> understand this might be if one thought of the idea of God's presence
> in all things. For example, because for Messiaen God is present in the
> added sixth chord as well as in the twelve-note constellation, he sees no
> problem in combining these disparate elements in one musical world.
> But a Messiaen added sixth chord is not just any old added sixth chord.
> Rather than being used, as in the Western tradition, as part of a chord
> progression in measurable and progressive time, it is adored and
> contemplated in the Now-moment of eternity....
>
> *Canteyojaya* is a huge mosaic of short sections: or else one might
> consider it an extremely complex verse-and-refrain form.... What is
> immediately apparent to the listener is how this fabric, like a Persian
> rug or a Byzantine mosaic, is full of absolutely gorgeous colors and

melodic turns. Messiaen's music alternately seems to evoke diamonds, bells, birds, flowers and stained-glass windows.

Vita, now more inspired by Vite than by Ishmael, also uses her writing to react to what she considers stylistic absurdities in certain conventional forms of writing. For about a year, just after brushing her teeth in the morning, she sat dutifully in our bedroom, which doubled as Bob's study, doing eye exercises to prevent near-sightedness. She picked books randomly off of Bob's shelves, perhaps Heidegger's *Being and Time* or Kant's *Critique of Pure Reason,* and alternately read a sentence and looked out the window at a distant tree in the park.

Whether she was training her eyes to adjust quickly or simply relaxing them after doing "close work," I never got straight, but in any case, over that year she absorbed a large dose of heavy philosophical writing. I suppose she could have discussed major philosophical issues with Bob over dinner, but she didn't. Instead, she produced a set of "philosophy papers" of her own that poked merciless fun, not only at Kant and Heidegger, but at her own father:

Me as an Existential Being

My self is a part of a universe of singular globes which revolve around me and which are the only things which make up heaven and earth and I am the thing that asserts itself above all other things and makes all other things seem like pluralities compared with me, and all other things which exist in the same position as I am in, as the only thing which exists and rules over all other things which, orally and otherwise, make up the universe at large, and all things that exist.

I have always envied the naive freedom Vita and Ishmael have taken with other people's language. Better to sound like Stevenson or even L.L. Bean, I figured, than like eight-year-old kids. But it was only much later that I realized how in making such free use of other writers' work, they were, in fact, using the work the way they used me: to begin to lay claim to their own writing.

As John Lampkin wrote,

The natural development of abstraction and reasoning from factual knowledge has its functional parallel in the development of a mature work function. For example, most great composers learned their craft by modeling their early works on the masterpieces (the facts) of their predecessors. As Stravinsky put it, "Great composers steal. Lesser composers borrow." And as Wilhelm Reich said about his early work with Freud in *The Function of the Orgasm,* "Unlimited devotion to a cause is the best prerequisite for intellectual independence."

Vita is perhaps too young yet to do anything but "steal," but just as Bach later "infused" in his concertos "the facile Italian style with a goodly dose of German counterpoint," Ishmael is now finding his original voice.

In the process, though, he has not been tempted to discard the conventional formal structures that he once intuited or later studied. Rather, just as John Holt felt that the structure and framework of the tennis court gave the game its challenge, Ishmael has continued to feel challenged and inspired by finding ways to work within given frameworks. As he wrote to a fellow composer:

> What I immediately see and hear in your piece I like a lot. I especially like how you were able to write a waltz that, without relinquishing its identity, was able to incorporate within itself some 2/4 measures. I am writing an opera just now which is largely dominated by the tango (which is actually danced through most of the first act) and, as a result, the music veers between absolutely straight 4/4 and 2/4, with ametric passages for relief, inspired by Persian music and Gregorian chant. This is just a different kind of effect, I guess. But it might be somewhat stunning if in the future progression of my opera a few 3/4 measures made an appearance.
>
> I was very intrigued by your letter in reaction to my response to your music. I, of course, agree that what one might call constructivism is a present danger. Perhaps a concrete situation to study with regard to the issue of technique would be Chinese and Japanese art. From what I have read, in China under the influence of Taoism and in Japan under the influence of Zen Buddhism, there was a huge cult of spontaneity and unselfconsciousness in art. But what that meant was that the artist spent years learning stereotyped forms which regulated the melodic patterns and their succession, for example, down to the last details, so that when inspiration struck, he or she could forget all that and create (and this is the same for haiku or flower arrangement) unselfconsciously, and yet follow every rule. Of course I am aware of the techniques that I am using, even at inspired moments, but what I am trying to imply is that perhaps intellection and inspiration are not antithetical.

A few months ago I read a book of lectures by Rabindra Nath Tagore, an Indian poet of the turn of the century, who in trying to describe the relation of the world to God used the metaphor of artistic creation, in which formless and infinite joy, or inspiration, is incarnated in limiting forms. The idea is that *joy and law go together.*

Math and Other Matters

"Do you remember the time," Vita asked me as we admired the three ripe blueberries on our new blueberry bush, "that Ishmael got this great scheme for making blueberry pies and selling them? But then we — it was us and the Nash-Graces — told you about it and you said that we should just sell the berries plain because people would like them better. We went to the Durhams but we couldn't decide what the price should be for each little basket and so we asked Mrs. Durham whether we should sell them for 25¢ or 40¢. She said 30¢ and bought one basket. Then we argued all the way home about how to divide the money four ways."

When Vita and Ishmael learned how to speak, and later to write and read, the materials they used "to build their own intellectual structures" were quite apparent. Often, though, the materials that Vita and Ishmael choose to build with, not to mention their actual methods of construction, are not nearly so obvious. Take Ishmael's music. He was already eight years old by the time we got around to arranging for him to have piano lessons.

"You know, of course, that he'll never be a professional musician," the teacher told me after the first lesson. "Most pianists start their formal training when they are four or five, or even younger. Horowitz 'played' on window panes when he was two; Rubinstein watched his older sister practice and could play all of her pieces by the time he was three. By the time they were Ishmael's age they were playing concertos."

To me, the naive mother, just hoping for a little cultural enrichment and fun for her kid, the piano teacher's supposed candor seemed uncalled for. It had never once crossed my mind that Ishmael might want to become a professional musician. (Actually, he was already writing music, then, but I didn't take it seriously. "He just likes drawing five-line staves and filling them in with little black dots," I told myself, with a lack of interest that now seems appalling. "But *that's* not writing music. There's just no way you can do that if you can't read it, much less play it.")

What was mainly on my mind as the piano teacher rattled on about Ishmael's missed opportunity was that after just this one lesson, it seemed obvious that Ishmael was so physically clumsy at the piano and his ear so bad (he couldn't tell a high note from a low note) that it wasn't going to make much difference whether he had started playing at three or eight or even twelve. The real question, it seemed to me then, was whether this supposed "cultural enrichment" was going to be worth the agony at all.

But there was no agony. By the time he was nine, Ishmael could name any note he heard, without seeing it played, and he could distinguish the notes in any three-note-chord or four- or five-note cluster. At ten he learned his first Mozart concerto.

By then I had read enough to know that the piano teacher had been "right." Great pianists (and violinists) invariably start young, and it isn't just that they begin their formal training at an early age, but that they routinely show a passionate interest in music from infancy.

Yet what about Ishmael? He had grown up with a piano; he had lived day in and day out with my amateurish plunking. Still he had never spontaneously learned any of my pieces. When the neighborhood kids hammered away on our piano he showed no interest. I don't know if he ever made a sound on it before he went to his first lesson.

The more musically accomplished and driven Ishmael became, of course, the more confused I felt about his apparent early musical indifference. Just what *was* Ishmael doing then, I used to wonder, searching for some kind of clue, like Horowitz's window panes. Could it have been the way he used to sing "She'll Be Comin' 'Round the Mountain" from the top of the jungle gym? Or all of the dancing that he and Vita did to our old jazz records? Maybe, and yet what really stood out in my mind, irrelevant as it then seemed, was Ishmael's absolute passion for the set of blocks that he had been given on his second birthday.

It had been those blocks, in fact, that had instantly changed his life (and mine). Instead of systematically tearing the house apart, which he had done routinely, and making messes in the kitchen —"Do you remember how I loved to cook?" he likes to remind me — now all he wanted to do was build. He spent hours each day sprawled on the floor with those blocks, building the most magnificent towers. He was never concerned with color and symmetry the way Vita later was, but he was fascinated by shapes and structures. His patience seemed endless, and for *such* a clumsy kid (he fell down twice during that period, gashing his head open and requiring stitches in the emergency room both times), the steadiness of his hands was remarkable as he placed blocks oh-so-carefully on top of one another.

At two and a half, Ishmael extended his building passion to the scrap lumber and tools in the shed. He now sawed, hammered, and nailed and at night he slept with his saw under his pillow. Now, too, he developed a horror of flat roofs ("thwat woofs," as he called them). He wouldn't enter a building unless he approved of the slope of the roof, and he would have nothing to do with Lego until I showed him how to make gabled roofs with the little Lego bricks. At three and a half, though he was still building passionately with blocks, mechanics and mechanical engineering became a competing passion. How does a car engine work? Ishmael wanted to know. How does an airplane fly?

In the shed he worked tirelessly, trying to build an airplane that would really fly. For Bob and me, meanwhile, it was a nightmare. Often I wished that he'd go back to cooking! Not only were three quarters of the nails he tried to hammer recalcitrant, but he consistently ignored our gentle reminders that in order to *really* fly, his airplane would need a real engine. Instead, he worked all the more fiercely, determined to design (and build) *his* airplane with just the right shape and proportions for maximum flight capability. Fortunately, he never got around to attempting a trial flight.

Ishmael built with blocks, messed around in the shed, and retained his firm architectural opinions right up until the time he began his piano lessons. Then, once again, everything changed. His tool chest gathered dust, and although he still built with Vita, the blocks served more than anything else as real building blocks for the purely functional houses they needed for their dolls.

Now it was the piano that preoccupied him. "Of course," I thought then, "Ishmael is growing up." Yet the more preoccupied he became with music, the guiltier I felt. I *hadn't* taken him to a piano teacher early and now it was too late. Ishmael, thanks to my negligence, could never have any hope of becoming a Rubinstein or a Horowitz.

But, of course, it wasn't too late (although Ishmael may never be a Rubinstein or a Horowitz) not only because, as John Holt said, "It's never too late," but because, as I finally figured out, Ishmael *had* been working on "music" right along — at least from the time those blocks entered his life, and maybe even earlier.

In order to speak music and interpret it, Ishmael has always had first to understand the way it is built. As I wrote earlier, it is the structure of the music that has always conveyed to him its essence. Could it have been, then, that he developed his ideas about structure concretely, by building, first with blocks and later with scrap lumber and old nails? Could it have been that in critically analyzing other people's buildings he developed a method that eventually gave him access to the world of organized sound, with its complex structures of melody, harmony, rhythm, and tone color?

I was so excited when I finally made these connections that I rushed to tell Ishmael. Naturally, being a bit overwhelmed, he just stood there, as if he needed time to think. Finally, he said rather tentatively, "Yeah, that makes sense. But you know, I just thought of something else, too. Do you remember how I was always playing war and planning out battles?"

"Sure," I said, remembering how his first grade teacher had told me that he was the most violent child she had ever met.

"Every time we went to the grocery store," he continued, now with more animation, "I imagined that the store was under attack and as we walked up and down the aisles I tried to visualize a strategy for defending it, usually with just you, me and Vita manning the defense.

"Sometimes I imagined battles taking place on the hills around our house, for instance, with my army in a defensive posture at the top of the hill, at an advantageous place, dug in behind breastworks made of lines of hay bales. That kind of format was typical of the Duke of Wellington's campaigns in Spain against Napoleon's generals."

Ishmael paused for a breath, now totally lost in thought, and then went on. "I was always reading about that sort of thing, remember? Well, anyway, the French generals made their armies charge up each hill in columns, a formation that limited their firepower drastically, Meanwhile, the Duke's troops would be securely on top, strung out in long thin lines, giving them full use of their firepower. You know, I was always running those kinds of battle formations through my head, working out slight strategical variants. I guess I was just fascinated by those kinds of tactical issues."

"I guess you still are," I couldn't help thinking.

"When we visited a place where the landscape was totally unpromising," Ishmael continued, the memories still pouring forth, "or when when we drove in the car, I would just turn inward and imagine naval battles (with sailing ships, of course) in which the direction of the wind relative to each ship was of paramount importance. In my mind, I always gave my captains tactical advantages, of course, moving them into position, say, so that they could give the enemy ship a broadside across the stern — raking the entire ship while the enemy was limited to responding with only one gun, located on the stern."

"Probably your teacher was convinced that you were going to grow up to be a psychopath," I told Ishmael. "Or do you think that she was more charitable and imagined you as a West Point graduate, even a general?" If I'd had to guess, though, I'm sure I would have thought immediately of the blocks and said, "Architect," or, much more tentatively, "Maybe an aerospace engineer, although I hope not. My nerves would never stand it!"

What would have happened, I've since wondered, if we had sent Ishmael to a piano teacher when he was three? Would he have been playing concertos at the age of seven or eight and composing sonatas? Or would he have been totally frustrated? Would he have lost interest in music or shown no interest in the first place, simply because our adult goals and expectations prevented him from doing the real work (building) that he felt that he needed to do?

Likewise, I've wondered what would have happened if Ishmael hadn't been given that set of blocks when he was two, or if Bob hadn't bought him a real saw and given him free rein with the scrap lumber in the shed. What if he simply hadn't had the initial "materials" that he needed in order to build for himself that entrance into the music world? Fortunately, as I've had to remind myself *often*, children are not only remarkably resilient, but ingenious at making use of *whatever* materials they discover — materials that we often overlook entirely.

Certainly, for years, perhaps because my own understanding of mathematics was so limited, I was at a loss to discover any materials around the house that Vita and Ishmael might use in order to learn math themselves. To use Seymour Papert's words once again, I was convinced that they were growing up in an impoverished, "math-poor environment." Everywhere I looked I saw books, typewriters, and piles of "in-process" manuscripts, but nowhere did I see a computer or even a calculator. We had an abacus but no one knew how to use it. We had no stop watch, no surveying equipment, and no paperback books of math puzzles.

In Michael Deakin's book, *The Children on the Hill,* which is the story of two parents raising four remarkable children (two of whom were math prodigies), he explains that the mother, Maria, retrieved the toys her babies threw out of their cots, over and over again, because she knew they were "exploring space and distance by judging the time that the toys took to fall to the ground." But while *she* retrieved the toys without complaint, marvelling at the ingenuity of not just her own children but all children, I wasn't nearly that perceptive. Instead, I always groaned, "Oh no, not again," as I bent over to pick up the plastic car keys that baby Ishmael pitched tirelessly onto the floor as he sat in his high chair. Later, I literally hired him to do the same job for baby Vita (thus firmly cementing their relationship, I soon realized). Yet never in a million years would it have occurred to me that they were happily doing math (and physics) together!

In line with what John Holt always said about how children learn best by exploring the real world, many homeschooling families I know write into their curriculums (if their school districts are at all likely to be sympathetic) that for math, their kids will be cooking, "halving and doubling recipes," and banking, "keeping careful accounts of their own money." I used to think it was great when these families actually managed to convince their superintendents that this was *real* math, but I myself wasn't so sure. To me, cooking and banking simply meant taking the easy way out — doing whatever possible to avoid family battles over math drills and flash cards.

Long ago, I had realized that I had learned essentially all the math I knew out in the real world, by cooking, balancing the checkbook, and figuring out the necessary sales tax when I ordered seeds by catalogue. Yet where, I wondered, had all that knowledge gotten me, other than a position as a competent housewife? I felt incompetent as a mathematician, not because there were math problems I met up with on a daily basis that I couldn't do, but because I felt that I *ought* to know at least some of the things that I imagined real mathematicians knew — how to multiply negative numbers or find square roots, for example. I wanted Vita and Ishmael to know those things too, but I was convinced, from my own experience, that you could never learn them in the ordinary course of events. And so, even when Vita and Ishmael were a long way off from having to multiply negative numbers or whatever (in terms of the usual school time frame), I was determined that our math curriculum would involve more than halving and doubling cups of sugar or counting up nickels and dimes.

As my friends all know, I used to explain away our math textbooks by shrugging my shoulders and saying, with a certain amount of embarrassment, since John's words always lingered in the back of my mind, "Well after all, we only have one cracked measuring cup in this whole house." Useless and even harmful as they often seemed, I didn't know how else to teach real math, except with a textbook.

In *Better Than School*, I wrote about how school, thanks mostly to the agony of the constant drill work, had wrecked whatever intuitive mathematical understanding Ishmael had once had. At home, as I described, he could spend an hour sitting over a problem like 3+4=? and not even realize that he could count on his fingers or line up three apples and four oranges from the fruit bowl and get the right answer by counting them. He could cut his birthday cake into eight fairly equal-sized pieces, but he had lost all sense of what the fraction 1/8 meant.

Every day we worked on math together from a pretty good textbook that we had found. We *never* pushed him to drill with flash cards or to do timed worksheets, yet at first, even with my arm lovingly wrapped around his shoulder, we often got through only one or two problems a day. Gradually, though, and this was very exciting to me, Ishmael began to relax around numbers. He learned how to add and subtract again (and how to count fruit), and he learned the principles of multiplication and division. He didn't actually manage to memorize his multiplication tables, though.

As I wrote in the book, "If you ask Ishmael an innocent question like, 'Who was Amerigo Vespucci?' he will bombard you with facts — the date and place of Vespucci's birth, the specifics of all of his ocean voyages, the date of his death, and so on. And then if, in amazement, you ask Ishmael when he last read up on Vespucci, he'll probably answer casually, 'Oh, about a year ago.' With a memory like that, you'd think he would have managed to memorize his multiplication tables in no time.... But somehow, they just won't stick in Ishmael's mind."

The past traumas lingered, and yet, considering what his school experience had done to him, he had become quite competent with numbers and I was pleased. Ishmael would never be a mathematician, I thought, but then you can't be everything, right? And besides, Vita, who was only five or six when I wrote that chapter on math, had never spent a day in her life hating math. "Give me some problems too," she used to beg as she worked with Ishmael at the kitchen table.

Yet even after she had learned to subtract negative numbers, find square roots, and calculate the measure of an angle, I wasn't satisfied. I still felt that something wasn't quite right — that this couldn't be what mathematics was or what mathematicians did. I knew that it was important for architects and orthodontists to be able to calculate the measure of an angle, but why me, or Vita and Ishmael, or any ordinary person, for that matter? Why even mathematicians? I kept wondering.

John Holt used to tell me patiently, "Math is fun."

"Yeah, for you," I thought, never quite convinced. I was sure that math must and should be something more than that, too. But what?

Seymour Papert was the one finally to set me on track, although not entirely in the way I expected. His book is about how children, with the aid of computers, can learn even the most abstract math. It didn't take me long to realize that when Papert used the word "math," though, he didn't mean multiplication tables or speed drills, or even calculating the measure of an angle. Mathematics, as he defined it, meant ways of exploring those very relationships in space and time that, as the mother Maria knew, babies are already beginning to be fascinated with. Although it took me longer to understand what this meant in terms of Vita and Ishmael's learning (and my own), one thing that became immediately clear to me was that all this time I'd been confusing simple everyday computation with mathematics.

That's where John Holt's "laws of nature" came in, I now saw. If what Vita and Ishmael needed was to become competent in our money-centered (cookbook-centered) society — not such a bad thing, when you think about it— then what they needed to learn were the skills necessary to do a little simple arithmetic. Yet how could a textbook or flashcards ever really convince them that when you take three from seven you get four? How could I ever expect them to memorize a fact like that if they had no conception of it? The only way, of course, for them to begin to conceive of it was to experience it by taking seven cookies, eating three, and discovering what happened; by cooking; and by spending money, much as my home-schooling friends proposed.

By defining mathematics as arithmetic, and then by taking arithmetic out of the realm of the everyday, school had given me the idea that if we could just sit long enough with the textbooks, we would eventually find ourselves doing what mathematicians did. Would we? In order to find my answer, I first had to figure out what "the everyday" meant. Was there really such a thing as a math-poor environment if even I had managed to learn basic calculation? Would I really have to invent activities for Vita and Ishmael to do — like cooking and banking— in order to make our environment math-rich? Did I need to go out and buy a new measuring cup?

With Papert's help, I was finally able to start looking at *our* environment. What I saw astonished me. Instead of finding *things* — measuring cups — I found *ways of using things,* things that were at hand, anything:

I am sitting in a cramped room watching Ishmael rehearse at a Yamaha grand with a violinist and a cellist. They are reading through the second movement of a Schumann trio. Suddenly, although his left hand continues to play arpeggios in regular triplets, Ishmael's face looks agitated and he begins tapping something, in mid-air, with his right hand. The violinist and cellist look up. "Your sixteenth is coming too late," Ishmael says. "It's sounding like a sextuplet. You should be playing it right after my third triplet. But don't listen to my part, just count sixteenths..."

We are out taking a walk. The sky is a deep blue and we can see for miles across a low valley to the rolling farm land beyond. Black-eyed susans, daisies, and clover line the roadside. Ishmael and Vita walk together up ahead. "Let's clap rhythms," says Ishmael. "You clap in fives and I'll clap in sixes. If we keep steady we should come together on every thirty beats." So much for the view and the wildflowers!

Rather shamefacedly, I realized that what John had told me was true. Math *can* be fun. But even more important, I realized that almost despite me, Vita and Ishmael had all along been quietly and contentedly using their *own* materials, picking and choosing from our environment like scavengers on a beach.

I remembered now that Ishmael had first discovered that fractions are division problems in a book of literature, not a math textbook, when he read the story of how Laura and Mary tried to divide two cookies three ways in *Little House in the Big Woods*. When he learned how to read music, he discovered that what's more, fractions merely represent the relationship between two numbers, and that even when the two numbers change — as when you transcribe a piece with a 4/4 time signature into 2/2 — it will only be a change in kind, not absolute value, since the relationship between the two numbers has remained unchanged.

Because Vita began studying music at such an early age, she literally grew up knowing this. She knew that in a 2/2 measure a half note gets one beat but that in a 4/4 measure, it's the quarter note that gets the beat. She knew, too, that if she set the metronome to 152 to the quarter note, it was the same as setting it to 76 to the half note, because what really mattered, she knew, was not whether she counted in quarter notes or half notes, but how the notes related, in time value, to the rest of the notes in the measure (what mathematicians call a ratio).

In addition, when, at the age of seven or eight, she began working on a piece that required her to play three notes in her right hand for every four in the left, she figured that the easiest thing to do was to find a common ground between both sets of notes, in this case twelve beats, and then count out the twelve beats as she played, a note with the right hand on every fourth beat and a note with the left hand on every third beat (common denominators).

Recently, Vita has been making three-dimensional toys out of folded paper, using one piece of paper for each toy, and cutting tabs with corresponding slits to hold them together. Since she works without a pattern, she first has to visualize the toy car or house or ball in her head, then imagine it as though cut apart, with all its various sides laid out flat. With the help of a ruler, she then transfers her mind's image to paper, making sure that all of her edges fit together like quilt pieces when she actually folds her paper into its final three-dimensional form (what mathematicians call spatial relationships, geometry).

Until they were about six or seven, or maybe even older in Ishmael's case, Vita and Ishmael refused to put their money in the bank because we couldn't assure them that if they put a dollar in they'd get the same dollar back. Over time, they learned (concretely, through the experience of handling money, and perhaps conceptually, just by playing music) that a dollar is a dollar, but that four quarters also make a dollar, as do ten dimes.

This was perhaps the most important lesson they ever learned, because only then could they really see that numbers have *both* fixed values and relative values. Only then could they understand, concretely, that a one in the tens place is the same as a ten in the ones place (borrowing and carrying), or that when we divide decimals it is fair to move the decimal in the divisor over to the right in order to create a whole number, as long as we move the decimal point over the same amount of spaces in the dividend.

All of this, of course, has to do with "place value" — a concept Ishmael's teacher had tried and failed to teach him in the first grade. But back then, he had no concrete models to fall back on. And *that* was exactly it, of course! Now I realized that when my friends proposed, in their curriculums, to do "kitchen math," as I had always thought of it skeptically, they were actually proposing to do far more than simply teach their kids how to add one cup plus one cup or how to divide one cup in half. Instead, by baking cakes and cookies, or doubling recipes for lasagna, their kids would eventually learn, just as Vita and Ishmael had learned, that, as I said before, numbers have both fixed values and relative ones. Only by understanding this would they ever begin to understand what numbers are all about.

Feeling excited by these discoveries of mine, I wrote to my friend Bill Hoyt, a mathematician, and told him about them. He wrote back to say:

> What you refer to as our over-emphasis on computation essentially boils down to an analogous obsession with the "grammar" of mathematics — the multiplication tables, the postulates of algebra and the axioms of geometry, even the method of long division taught in *this* textbook as opposed to *that* one — to the exclusion of any clue as to what all this stuff is actually *good* for, what makes it interesting. It's as though some misguided physical education instructor decided to teach his charges to play baseball by sitting them down at desks for a couple of years to study the rules (with weekly multiple-choice spot quizzes on such key vocabulary words as 'inning' and 'earned run average'), then another couple of years working out conventions and strategies ('With two outs and runners on first and second, the third baseman should (a) shade right (b) shade left (c) play deep (d) move in for the bunt (e) not enough information') before he ever let them out on the field to see what in the world they were doing all this work for.

What Bill was saying, of course, was just what John Lampkin had said when he wrote that in school, "abstraction and reasoning, instead of being a natural outgrowth of factual knowledge, become displaced." If we never allow kids out on the field, memorizing the rules of baseball will never give them a sense of the game or any desire to play it.

Arithmetic is essentially like housework. It really is a part of our everyday environment, as Vita and Ishmael showed me — so much so, in fact, that I now know that if we don't actively prevent our children from going out on the field, we never need think in terms "allowing" them out. It simply happens, the way learning to make beds or wash dishes happens.

When Ishmael, and later Vita, turned eleven or twelve, multiplication "just happened": one day they still didn't know their multiplication facts, the next day they did. In Vita's case the process was painless.

"I don't even remember trying to learn them," she says. "All I know is that I got sick of counting on my fingers. It took too long. When I stopped, I discovered that I didn't need to anyway."

With Ishmael, thanks to my expectations, both spoken and unspoken, the process wasn't what I'd call painless, but it was certainly dramatic. He had agonized over his multiplication tables for years, running through one gimmick after another in his attempts to memorize them. He had even drilled himself with the dreaded flash cards, as if hoping that if nothing else, the agony would be good for him. "Passable," however, was about all we could call the fruits of his labor.

Then one Christmas he decided to buy his presents mail-order, and he discovered that he needed to multiply the prices of several different items in order to figure out how much money he was going to have to make his check out for. I could tell that he dreaded having to count everything out on his fingers. It wasn't just the humiliation, it was, as with Vita, the time involved. He spent a while looking around for his multiplication chart— his usual crutch— but he couldn't find it. Finally, he took a pencil and a deep breath, and simply sat down to face his order blank. As if willing the answers, he found himself multiplying 5x9 and 8x7.

Arithmetic, though, is not simply math facts. Arithmetic is a set of tools people use to help them anticipate the reactions of certain kinds of actions in the real world— like what happens when you start out with seven cookies and eat three of them. Unfortunately, most of us never have a chance to discover this. In his article in the *Whole Earth Review*, "Let's Eliminate Math From Schools," Roger Schank writes, "Schools believe in teaching the answers, and children brought up on formulaic thinking begin to believe that there is an answer to every question." In other words, they are taught not to think in terms of tools, but in terms of automatic solutions.

When Ishmael was in first grade, he learned to think of numbers simply as answers to be pulled out of thin air. "3+4 is um... um... oh yeah, seven." Regardless of whatever mathematical intuition he might have brought with him to school, he was a failure at school math because he was no good at conjuring up right answers. Yet at home, when I suggested to him that he might like to take a break from his textbook and spend a few weeks playing with Cuisenaire rods (colored wooden rods of various metric lengths), he rebelled. He figured that if he was going to have to learn "math" (i.e. math facts), he might as well do it and not waste time fooling with little blocks. He had a point.

In his new book, *Learning All The Time*, John Holt writes, "There is no such *thing*, or mathematical idea, as 'infinity.' There is just the adjective 'infinite,' meaning... without an end or an edge." Similarly, there is no such *thing* as mathematics. Mathematics is a verb — a way of looking at the world. Arithmetic provides the set of tools that can often help us look — although not always. John had said that math is fun. Bill Hoyt said, later on in his letter, that he used math as a way to "think systematically," to "focus on increasingly complex patterns of thought." But it was Aaron Falbel, in a paper called "The Mathematics of the Ordinary," who most helped me to make the important connections. "Mathematics," he wrote,

> is a *human endeavor* — it's what mathematicians do. The stuff that ends up in the textbooks is the result of their work. Similarly, the black lines and dots that musicians read are not themselves music, though we often call them that. Music is what the people are *doing*.... Both mathematics and music are activities. One *does* mathematics. One *makes* music....
>
> We are everywhere surrounded by pattern, patterns of shape, of motion, of language, of behavior, of sound, of history... of practically anything that has a *form* of one sort or another. The act of perceiving, recognizing, classifying, describing, capturing, analyzing, mulling over, or playing with patterns involves a type of *formal thinking* that lies at the heart of... mathematics.

Mathematics, I have learned, is at once something that mathematicians do and something that babies do, like Maria's children, and Vita and Ishmael, when they dropped toys on the floor time and time again. Mathematics is exactly what Vita and Ishmael so often did in their fantasy play and in music. At the same time, for Ishmael to take out the textbook and set to work, to decide not to play with Cuisenaire rods but to stick to flash cards and drill, was for him to cut himself off from the harmony of numbers, to learn arithmetic at the price of mathematical ignorance, abandonment. Only by living in the world, reflecting on it and, among other things, playing music, could Ishmael have mathematics returned to him.

I blame myself, and yet there was nothing more difficult for me than trusting Vita and Ishmael to build their "intellectual structures" out of materials that at first so totally eluded me. Even with the best intentions, even as I suggested distance from the textbook by offering Cuisenaire rods instead, I was limiting Vita and Ishmael's ability to perceive, intuitively, concrete relationships between numbers and to make abstractions from those numbers. By offering specific materials to them, and suggesting ways those materials could be used, I was inadvertently limiting their whole notion of what looking at the world as a mathematician might mean.

Using Teachers

Calvino: I'M NOT A GARDENER, I'm a teacher.

Peter: Calvino, the way people are teachers here is by doing what they're going to teach, not by "teaching."

Lloyd: If you start doing something and if you love your work, if you're really into it, people will come and help you out.

Peter: And if nobody'll help you, just go ahead and do it anyway, because it seems the nature of all the staff here is that they're going ahead and doing what they're into. And if the students come along, fine, and if they don't, that's fine too. It's not as if we're really teachers here. Ann's an artist and she goes right ahead with what she IS. It's really true. Martin's a musician; he doesn't stop because nobody happens to come that day.

Calvino: Man, if I'm going to be a gardener I can go out and make 500 bucks a month being a gardener. I don't want to be a gardener. I want to be a teacher, man.

Lorna: You should teach by doing the thing that you're teaching.

— Fragments from a discussion among staff and students at Pacific High School, transcribed in the book, *The Teacher Was The Sea*, by Michael S. Kaye

Susan Richman, editor of the newsletter *Pennsylvania Home-schoolers,* responded to the portion of my last chapter that appeared in *Growing Without Schooling* by writing:

> I think Bill Hoyt may have missed a chance to open up math thinking in another way for Nancy. He never mentioned the *history* of mathematics as being a source of interest to a non-math type of person, a way of beginning to look at mathematics with new eyes. It's an approach we have always used around here with Jesse and Jacob, and I have learned so much right along with the kids. Suddenly math, and even just "simple" arithmetic, becomes a long time-line of fascinating *people* who tried, and tried hard, to make sense of their world with the best of their minds and the best tools of their times. It's no longer just stuff put in textbooks and achievement tests....
>
> Studying math history is indeed one of the fine ways to view history (maybe better than the war-rulers-vanquished approach) — it is not separate from the rest of the problems, or ideas, or the people of its time. We love reading about Pythagoras and his mystic group of students inventing numerology lore along with their concrete discoveries of triangle and square numbers and prime numbers and hypotenuses of right triangles. We're touched reading about Archimedes asking a conquering Roman soldier, about to run him through with a sword, to please wait just a minute so that he can finish the geometrical proof he was working out in the sand with a pointed stick....

More than just offering me a new way to look at mathematics, Susan's response was a gentle reminder to me that children, like adults, want to know, not just how to play the piano or add up birthday checks, but how other people actually work — what they have invented, built, and thought about. Children want to know what questions people have asked in the past and what answers they came up with, not because they care about ancient history as an academic subject but because it is a way for them to get *inside* the human work that has gone into making the world what it is. We must not, Susan was saying, overlook *people,* the creators and conveyors of our culture, as important building materials for our children to use.

Perhaps she was too polite to say so outright, but I think she was implying something else, simply by describing her reading sessions with Jesse and Jacob. Although I know that she agrees with me, implicitly, that we must allow our children room to make their own discoveries and to draw their own conclusions — to own their learning process — she was reminding me, by example, that as with Vita and Justin we must not deny or underestimate our own role in that process. I *still* read to Vita and Ishmael every day, I *still* edit their writing critically, and I *still* peek in at Vita and say, "Hey, I think that phrase needs a bigger crescendo to the top," or "I'd like to see a more relaxed bow hold." As parents, and as friends to children, we are, both as role models and as active teachers, perhaps the *most* important building materials they have.

There are many different ways, of course, that children can use us as they go about building their own intellectual structures. I remember bringing baby Ishmael home from the hospital and realizing, with a kind of terror, "My God, he doesn't know that nighttime is when *we* sleep!" Yet by sharing our bed at night, he quickly learned the meaning of a civilized sleep schedule — not that he instantly chose to embrace civilization, but that's another story! By sitting at the table with us and having free access to forks and spoons and yes, even table knives, he learned how to spoon up peas and butter bread and he quickly learned to wipe his face and hands with a napkin, just the way we did. He learned to talk by listening to us talk and by being included in our conversations, and he learned how to pee in the potty by watching us, by noticing that big people did not wear diapers.

Those were the passive ways we taught Ishmael, and all parents teach their children, simply by including them in life's activities. But although I don't underestimate the importance of that kind of teaching, I agree with Susan Richman that not only were we Ishmael's active teachers as well, but that we should have been. We actively taught Ishmael that the world is a loving, responsive place when I nursed him at his slightest whimper or Bob held him in his arms. We actively taught him how to straighten bent nails when he worked on his airplane in the shed; we taught him to ride a bike when we ran up and down the road, steadying the back wheel of his bike as he pedalled madly and tried to balance himself; we taught him to love literature when we snuggled up on long winter nights to read *Winnie-the-Pooh* and other old favorites; and we taught him how to care for plants when we showed him how to trowel on the manure as we set out tomato seedlings in the spring.

Just as with Susan Richman, whose own enthusiasm held her kids' attention as much as or more than the people they were reading about, so did our enthusiasm hold Ishmael's attention when we read to him or worked with him in the shed or out in the garden. As much as they want to know anything, children want to know what *we* genuinely care about. They expect and demand honesty from us as their teachers.

Susannah Sheffer wrote in a letter to me:

Have I told you that Amanda Bergson-Shilcock (ten and a half, now) has been sending me, intermittently throughout this past fall, a story she's been working on? I make comments and she revises the story and sends me the next draft. When I was visiting her family over the holidays, she specifically asked to work with me, and I was quite taken aback by how ready she had become, in the months since I'd seen her, for intensive work on a piece. She was able to accept criticism, to think about how the thing should sound. I'd start to say something and she'd interrupt, 'Yes, yes, how about —' Working with her was truly exhilarating....

It was so easy to respond authentically, to speak as a writer rather than as a teacher, and I am astonished by my understanding, or re-understanding, that teaching can only be teaching of a *particular* thing. You know John Holt said to people who want to "work with children," find something that's worth doing and find ways to let children help you. Well, it's easier to think of that in terms of building a house or working for nuclear disarmament. It seems almost sinfully delightful to work with a young person on something that you just, simply, love, but can't justify — and don't need to justify, because the young person's desire to join you provides the justification (so it is, partly, selfish). But think how different this is from some vague enthusiasm for "teaching." When I think about that, I don't know what it means. I don't think it *can* mean anything that isn't dishonest. Teaching that pretends to be anything but a presentation of one's concerns and passions is dishonest....

For as long as I've know him, my father has taught what I grew up thinking of as "Poly Sci I" to hundreds of college freshman each year. Lecturing has always seemed to be an instinctive part of his nature. As a child, I remember watching him pace up and down the room one long, rainy afternoon as he lectured to me about his hero, Martin

Luther. I still remember the picture that grew in my mind as he spoke, of Luther nailing up the Ninety-five Theses on the church door — a picture so vivid, in fact, that it blotted out every sense I had of the gray day outside and the drops of rain sliding down the window panes. (But I also remember that when I was "bad," I would pray silently to myself, "Please, please, *just* spank me." My father's moralistic lectures were dreadful when he directed them at me!)

When he comes to visit here, he gives Vita and Ishmael lectures. Sitting with Vita on the couch, he tells her, in that slow, careful lecturing tone of his, about the virtues of Monet's painting as opposed to Manet's. As we walk through a rhododendron garden in full bloom he lectures Ishmael about the failure of Congress to draw up legislation to clarify disputes between the states over their off-shore territorial claims.

"You see," I hear him say, "it's just that kind of failure to deal with potentially touchy political issues that causes fiascos like 'Irangate.'"

Always when I hear my father lecture like that, I half expect Vita and Ishmael to back away (politely), eyes glazed over with boredom, like the kids I remember from school when our teachers lectured us. But not so! Always, they surprise me by asking their grandfather for more. As Susannah's young writer friend was by her — as I was on that far off rainy afternoon — Vita and Ishmael are drawn in by my father's concerns and passions, by his honest giving of himself.

Here I think, too, of John Holt in one of the stories I told about him in the memorial article that I wrote for *Mothering*:

> One afternoon, while John was snoozing on the couch, Vita and I decided to do a little math. (No, I still hadn't learned my lesson!) We had just started learning how to divide fractions and as luck would have it, Vita asked me *why* it was, anyway, that when all you were really trying to do was divide fractions, you not only had to take the second fraction and turn it upside-down, but then you had to multiply and *not* divide, which was what you were supposed to be doing in the first place. The textbook that we were using had some sort of confusing explanation that made us both more confused than ever, and finally, since Vita was tired anyway, she burst into tears. (A homeschooler's nightmare, I couldn't help thinking — to make your kid cry over a math problem right in front of John Holt!)
>
> John could never bear to hear children cry, and his eyes popped open with Vita's first sobs. "What's the trouble, Lambkin?" he asked.

She was in no mood to answer and so I said, "Oh, it's nothing really. We shouldn't have tried to divide fractions when she was to tired." "Maybe I can help," he said. "Let me look at the book." Well, I couldn't help thinking that now we were in for real trouble. Vita was red in the face and she looked as if she wasn't about to let anybody try to tell her anything. Dutifully, though, she gave John the book, and sat down next to him. He looked over it and then spent some time just staring off into space while Vita looked at him curiously. Then he began talking to himself and scribbling on a piece of paper. Vita watched, and listened, and gradually John began directing his talk to her, almost as if she was just an extension of himself. And she, meanwhile, was becoming totally involved in what he was doing, which was trying to work out a simple proof to answer her question. By the time he had actually worked it out, Vita was right with him, and I think they were both equally thrilled. "Pleased as punch," as he used to say.

Children lose interest in us as teachers as soon as we make ourselves mere passive conveyors of knowledge, like most teachers in school, who try *not* to reveal their own personal biases and passions for fear of unduly influencing their students and preventing them from learning to think objectively. But children *want* us to reveal ourselves to them. Just as important, they want and need to be able to reveal their own feelings, ideas, and personal biases to us. Just as when we invite children to share in our pleasures and enthusiasms, so we play an important role as their teachers when we listen to them and take their ideas seriously. Only then can they actively test out their ideas against honest and thoughtful responses. Children need us, as their teachers, to "push against," as Susannah once put it.

Ishmael and Vita use us that way all the time (as Bob and I use each other and even the kids), but they also use other people. Last summer, for example, while he was playing at a music festival in Vermont, Ishmael had one such "back and forth" with the co-director of the festival as she drove him home from a concert. Simply by listening and responding to Ishmael, she brought out, in his thinking, new ideas that kept his mind active and fertile for months afterwards. He transcribed the conversation into his notebook when he came home so that he would never lose it (omitting, as he told me, the long pauses that he took in order to work out his ideas or at least make them coherent):

Janet: One of the violists was telling me the other day that the two composers we had with us this summer sounded as if they had come straight out of the 1940s.

Ishmael: Yes, I think that's right. It's so neat, everybody was getting so desperate in the 1950s and 1960s — it's like everybody was going to all these extremes. Because on the one hand there were the absolute-control-of-music people, which eventually became electronic music — I mean it's so amazing, you can control everything about the sound — and then there were all these chance experiments, and improvisation and stuff.

Janet: Is that like John Cage?

Ishmael: Yeah, he was one of them.

Janet: You know, he's coming next year as our guest composer.

Ishmael: Yes, that's so exciting!

Janet: I've heard so many different things about him. Some people say his music is really lovely, and then others say that he's arrogant and you can't talk to him.

Ishmael: Well, he's done so many different things so they might have heard different things. But the connecting link is Zen Buddhism. He's been a Zen Buddhist for a long time and so, you know, you can't call him arrogant, because he doesn't believe in himself as an individual; it's just this strange relationship that the Zen people have to the public. A week before I came here, I was talking to an experimental composer who was really inspired by Cage's music, and he said that what he learned from Cage was that music didn't have to be organized like language, you know, with grammar and so forth —

Janet: So not tonal, in other words?

Ishmael: Yes, well, tonal chords could come in, but they wouldn't have to resolve in certain ways. And there's also the idea that all sound is music. John Cage is not that interested in communication, because he thinks that you can't express reality through language.

Janet: Even in music?

Ishmael: No. I agree with Cage that I don't really think you can. I think music is like these persons that we come into contact with — like a part of reality, not an expression of it.

Janet: But music is so human! Do animals have music? Trees and stones? No!

Ishmael: Well, they might have something else which we wouldn't recognize. But it's true, only humans have music.

Janet: I think that all of our human relations go into music.

Ishmael: But it's just so hard to explain how that happens. I mean, nobody ever has. We have emotional reactions to music, but —

Janet: Our ears must be so amazing. This is something I often ponder — how can these *tones* convey to us such a feeling of hope —

or hopelessness?

Ishmael: Yes, I wonder about that too. A lot of it must have to do with expectations. You expect that certain things are going to happen, and either they do, or your expectations are frustrated. If they are frustrated consistently, that would, I guess, produce the feeling of hopelessness, and if they look like they are going to be fulfilled, that would be your hope. It's the same in music as in real life. I mean, so often our expectations lead to disappointment and sorrow. Yet if we were absolutely detached from the world — even if we had no sorrows — that would be terrible. I'm convinced that we were born into the world in order to live in it and be attached to it, and if attachment to other people and things gives us sorrow, all that means is that happiness is not the absolutely most important thing in life.

In *How Children Learn* John Holt wrote, "We do not ask or expect a child to invent the wheel starting from scratch. He doesn't have to. The wheel has been invented. It is out there, in front of him... A child does not need to be *told* what wheels are and what they are for in order to know. He can figure that out for himself, in his own way, in his own good time. In the same way, he does not have to invent the electric light bulb, the airplane, the internal combustion engine — or law or government, art or music. They, too, have been invented and are out there. The whole culture is out there. What I urge is that a child be free to explore and make sense of that culture in his own way."

As with all of the materials that children choose to build with, children must be free to use us "in their own way," as John said, and only at times that make sense to them. Ishmael had the absolute freedom to mull over his conversation with Janet in his mind in whatever ways he chose, *or* to forget it. When my father lectures Vita and Ishmael, they know that they *can* back away. They can question him, and what's more, they can disagree with him (although he makes a formidable opponent). When the adult expectations are very clear, as in encounters like these, Vita and Ishmael know that they are free to use (or not use) the materials that they have been offered in whatever ways they please, no matter how opinionated the adults might be.

How different, though, from the time that I suggested to Ishmael that he might like to "play" with Cuisenaire rods, hoping, of course, that he would learn how to add and subtract. By having a specific, but unspoken, goal for him in the back of my mind — even though I didn't actively insist upon it and genuinely wanted him to play, as well — I manipulated and confused the issue and so robbed him of the freedom that was rightfully his. If Susan Richman had read math history to Jesse and Jacob because she hoped that they would then attack their math textbooks with more enthusiasm, knowing now what math is good for, then she, too, would have been stealing from her kids.

And yet while we, in our better moments, do what we can to allow our children the freedom they need to discover and explore the world about them, there is no need, as John said, to ask or expect them to invent the wheel. It is, after all, already "out there."

When Bob says to Vita and Ishmael, "Sure, you guys can chop wood, but only if you're wearing boots and *only* if you set up your chopping blocks at opposite ends of the pile so that you don't hit each other with your axes or get hit by stray chips," he means, "This is how I learned to chop wood safely. There is no need for you guys to invent safe ways to do it yourselves, although you are welcome to, but for the most part, anyway, *that* culture has already been invented."

Yet within the "cultural" structure that Bob has laid out, are Vita and Ishmael still free to make their own discoveries? Have issues of safety limited their freedom? And if so, does it matter? From watching Vita and Ishmael work in the woodpile, I never doubted their continual sense of discovery. They discovered, by trial and error, that oak splits more easily than maple, for example, and that the lower down you grasp the ax handle the more power you can put into your swing. They discovered ways to gauge which way the chips would fly, often by theorizing about the possible results first and then designing experiments to prove or disprove their theories. Vita discovered counting in the woodpile, and she learned that twelve long, fat logs of Bob's took longer to burn than twelve short, skinny ones of hers.

Yet what about safety? Although it's tempting to tell ourselves that in matters of life and death, questions of freedom are irrelevant, I think, now, that the issue is far more complex. It's an issue that I continue to ponder, and am only just finding answers to. In the woodpile, for example, I wonder if the situation didn't work out as well as it did only because Bob was working seriously himself and *never* asked Vita and Ishmael to observe points of safety that he himself did not observe; because in the matter of safety, as in everything else, he was honestly sharing his work with them. Real work represents *process*, movement, and perhaps because Bob's safety standards were so much a part of his work they never implied arbitrary, rigid law to the kids, but rather a part of his open and straightforward invitation to them to join in the fluidity of his work.

Are we offering our children the same kind of open invitation when they decide to trust their money to a bank or keep their accounts straight or pass the math section on a standardized test and we show them how to write down and figure their numerical calculations on paper? Wouldn't it be a total waste of time, and in a sense an outright rejection of them, if we expected our children to work out their own methods of calculating? Like John's electric light bulb or airplane, hasn't the wheel of arithmetic already been invented?

When Vita was ready to go to the bank, I told myself that just as she had spent hours in the woodpile kibbitzing with Bob and had, in effect, learned how to chop wood before she ever held a hatchet in her hands, so, as she handed her money over to the bank teller, she already knew — primitively, but a least in principle — how to add and subtract. I was sure that to sit down with her and show her how to line up sums on paper, how to add from right to left, and how to borrow and carry, could only cement her knowledge of the wheel, not interfere with her own sense of the process. I imagined that my help was a way of saying, "Writing down and solving arithmetic problems this way is a part of our inherited culture, a practical tool that adults use every day, and one that you will surely find useful too."

It didn't occur to me that I might be wrong until I read a piece by Maggie Sadoway about her son, Solon, in *Growing Without Schooling* #63. "I am reluctant," she wrote,

> to ask Solon many questions about his methods of doing arithmetic for fear of tampering with his elegant system of teaching himself. I do know that he's had lots of experience with money: at our store, with his personal purchases and bank account, and through his twice-a-year used toy sales where he regularly takes in over $100. (He keeps track of the original price he pays for the toys, adds on the sales tax he paid, subtracts 40% with a calculator, then rounds off the answers to find the amount he wants to sell them for.) I also know that he sees us use numbers a lot and that he's never been given reason to think arithmetic is hard or beyond him. Once in a while, because he knows I'm interested, he'll share with me how he's gotten a certain answer. A few

examples: "600 drachmas must be \$4 because 300 drs. is \$2." "9+7. Nine is 2 more than 7. So put 1 on the 7, that's 8+8=16." "Five 15's are 75? Oh, yes, of course, because 20 fives are 100 and five 5's less would be 75."

Maggie goes on to say that only if you believe, as the schools do, that there is one right way to do arithmetic, does it make sense to teach it.

> Solon can easily add numbers such as 47+58, but he doesn't do it the "proper" way. (Even the proper way depends on what year you were born or what culture you live in. Solon has discovered it is much easier to add 29+48 if you think of it as 30+50 minus the 3 you just added on. In Greece I have seen children taught that method in school but as far as I know it is not common in this country.) Solon solves problems by using a system he's figured out for himself, one that truly makes sense to him. My guess is that in the process he's made his knowledge about numbers his own, a permanent part of his life, in a way that would be the envy of any school program.

I now see that unlike Bob, with his safety rules in the woodpile, by teaching Vita methods for calculating on paper, I was, in fact, excluding her from the process, the work of mathematics. I was laying down rigid law, so to speak, by implying through my teaching and my own lack of imagination, that there was only one right way to solve problems. In doing so I cut Vita off from her own sense of discovery by implying, "There is nothing to explore. There is no wilderness here, only civilized terrain." Perhaps that's why she eventually turned to music to explore mathematics — it was the one frontier left open to her.

As active teachers of our children, we also have to consider the question of boundaries as we share their work or invite them to share in ours. How do we draw the line between entering into and supporting our children's enthusiasms and overpowering them with our own? When Vita comes to me and says, "I need help 'cause I want to make only half this cake so that I can bake it in my little pan but I can't figure out what half of 3/4 is," and I say, "Well, the easiest thing to do would be to guess by the way it looks on the measuring cup. I mean, there's no need to be absolutely precise. But then again, it might be fun if we *did* try to work it out. If we turned the quarters into eighths, like this...", am I overstepping my bounds?

Was I overstepping my bounds when Vita said, "I want to learn to play Bach minuets," and I, in my enthusiasm, offered her snacks as enticements to practice well enough so that she really could have a chance of learning them?

John Holt, who visited us often with his cello, used to tell me, "*Never* think in terms of practicing. Simply *playing* is enough." And yet I knew that in order to play Bach well, disciplined work — practice — was essential. Practice is, after all, one of the most basic elements of musical culture, and as I tried to remind John, he had said himself, "We do not ask or expect a child to invent the wheel starting from scratch.... The whole culture is out there."

Our caring and experienced piano teacher, Bob Fraley, used to smile at Vita when she said stubbornly, "I already know how to play the piano. All you do is hit the keys!" Quoting Shinichi Suzuki he would tell her, "Only practice on the days you eat." Fraley told Vita that if she was old enough to sit at the table and eat three meals a day — if she was old enough to brush her teeth, for God's sake — then certainly she was old enough to do some careful work on "Twinkle, Twinkle Little Star." I agreed.

As I described in *Better Than School,* our trials and tribulations over Vita's practicing were anything but easy. Yet by five and a half, she could not only play those minuets with grace, but she now worked hard at the violin, too. ("I want to play THAT!") John used to ooh and aah over Vita's accomplishments — just as he oohed and aahed at the great playing that he heard at Boston Symphony concerts each week — and yet when he said, "Never think in terms of practicing," it was as if he assumed that her music simply appeared out of thin air, like magic.

Actually, watching John at our house as if in preparation to do some serious musical work — setting up his music stand, tuning his cello (and that could take an hour of messing around, just by itself), opening his music and putting on his glasses — I often wondered if he knew what serious work was. Usually, despite the glasses and the opened music, he just played away to himself, mostly sad, haunting melodies high up on his A string.

But I knew, of course, that John *did* know what serious work was. He had written almost a dozen books, after all. I knew, too, that he knew that children, like Vita, were perfectly capable of doing serious work themselves. One day he told me passionately, "It's such a sad thing! Most adults simply refuse to believe that children ever work hard unless they are somehow forced to. They look at a bunch of kids playing out on the basketball court summer day after summer day and they think, 'Those lazy bums. They should be mowing lawns or bagging groceries, earning a few bucks to save for college.' But what they don't see is that those very kids work harder in a day then we do in a week. Look at the beads of sweat dripping off their foreheads. Look at the taut muscles in their legs as they leap for a basket, with the elegance, almost, of dancers. Look at the intensity in their eyes as they follow the ball around the court."

With Vita, though, it only took one look between them for me to know that he meant *anything* but hard work — "Hey, let's go off and have some fun!" John's grin was both alluring and infectious. Off they'd go, with violin and cello in tow, often for a couple of hours at a stretch, and settle themselves "seriously" (they had to tune up, you know) out under the maple tree, or perhaps in John's room.

Amidst Vita's squeals and John's low chuckles and murmers, I heard them sliding their fingers up and down their fingerboards, making wild fire engine sounds. When Vita made high, squeaky sounds, way up at the tippy-top edge of her fingerboard, I heard John cheer, as if she had just mastered the highest notes of the Mendelssohn concerto. Sometimes Vita went to the piano. "Ah, how like Horowitz!" he might cry, as her fingers made huge crashing leaps. And once, when they were fooling around together, he said thoughtfully, "You know, we're beginning to sound, oh, just a wee bit, like Emmanuel Ax and Yo-Yo Ma."

I thought John was crazy (and all the more so when there *was* that touch of seriousness in his voice!), but I couldn't help but love and appreciate the sense of musical delight that filled the house when he was around. (Yes, disciplined work *was* important, I thought, but...) He gave Ishmael a copy of Beethoven's sonatas for cello and piano— some of the greatest music ever written — and together they muddled through the A major sonata. He gave us all an edition of the Mozart piano quartets, convinced me to get out my old viola, and showed Vita and Bob (who had just started learning the cello) how to pick out whatever notes they could while still keeping up with the rest of us.

We went to concerts together and always sat in the front row because John said that the music sounded best when you could see the sweat on the performer's brow, and he taught Vita and Ishmael how to yell "Bravo! Bravissimo!" with abandon. After dinner he used to tell us stories about musical disasters — "Have I told you about my cellist friend who was touring with a large orchestra and actually fell off the stage as they were playing—now let's see, what *was* that piece? — because the stage was too small?" But he also told very serious stories about the concerts he heard every week at the Boston Symphony — "The tears just rolled down my cheeks when they played the last movement of the Mahler."

All along, I was convinced that the musical fun and delight that John injected into our lives gave Vita and Ishmael a much needed breather from the hard work they did every day on music. But especially in Vita's case, I decided, it actually provided the balance she needed to be able to do that work at all — work that she seemed more and more determined to do.

Slowly, now, she was learning how to make musical sense of her pieces and to care about her sound. And like Ishmael, she was developing her own ideas about how to practice. If I said, "Why don't you play the passage five times," she might say, "*That's* not going to help. My problem is bringing out the melody line. I think I ought to first play all of the voices separately a few times so that I can really hear them."

"She has taken on such a big burden," I often thought, now grateful for John's infectious grin.

As time went by, though, I realized that John's fun had been far more than *just* fun. When Vita now slid her hand up easily to the end of her fingerboard in a deBeriot concerto, it was clearly because she had been doing that for years with John, "for fun." When she now dashed off a cadenza in a Mozart concerto — not as cleanly as Horowitz, but certainly in the spirit — it was because, thanks to John, she had been impersonating Horowitz for just as many years.

Yet John gave Vita still more — something that I never properly recognized until after he had died, when Vita was ten and Ishmael just fourteen. That winter, Vita had a chance to play, for a weekend, in an orchestra made up of high school students from around the state. The guest conductor for the event was Carl St. Clair, the new assistant conductor of John's beloved Boston Symphony. As I sat in the auditorium during rehearsals, I kept thinking how much John would have given to be there with me — not just because Vita was "sitting under the baton," as I'm sure he would have put it, of the BSO's assistant conductor, but because of St. Clair himself.

Up on the podium (yes, sweat drenching his shirt) he was so expressive with his body and so precise with his hands. And the way he seemed to draw the sound out of the orchestra reminded me of a pianist drawing the sound from all eighty-eight keys of the piano. He knew exactly what he wanted to do with the music and so much of the time the rehearsals were just a series of stops and starts.

"Play these notes at the very tip of your bow and way out on the fingerboard," he said, "or you're never going to get the kind of eerie sound I want." Or, "Give these notes a sense of direction the way a singer would. You need to give shape to the line or it will just die."

Scattered throughout the auditorium were high school music teachers and they, like me, were amazed at the music that was pouring out of those kids. There was St. Clair, dancing around, and with every word and gesture he drew the music out. "Music without risk," he said, "is nowhere! You've got to go for the maximum!"

As he said that I heard the teacher next to me whisper, "That's what we've been saying all along to our kids but they don't listen. They just continue to play like three year olds."

Suddenly it was if I had heard a voice from my past — my own school music teacher — shouting to our little orchestra, "Come on now, stop playing like three year olds!"

To say that, I realized, was to say, "I am your teacher and I know what is best for you." But when St. Clair said, "Never think about cutting off a note. Instead, imagine how you want the silence to sound," he never meant to imply, as an ordinary teacher might have, "Play the music the *right* way." Rather, with every word and gesture he was telling the kids, "It is my job as conductor to interpret the music and your job as instrumentalists to play it." With every word and gesture St. Clair invited the kids to join him in his work.

It was then that it first dawned on me that John had been doing the same thing when he grinned alluringly at Vita and took her off to make strange noises in the bedroom. "This is *my* work," his grin implied. "Join me."

Like St. Clair, I now realized, John *was* a working musician. He was a real musical experimenter and innovator. Even as he messed about with Vita he was experimenting with his sound or figuring out new ways to work on technical problems. The spontaneity of music fascinated him. John, I realized, was the first *working* musician Vita had ever known. He had no desire to make her into a well-rounded musician, and in fact, as I was well aware, he made no bones about revealing his personal biases to her ("Never think in terms of practicing"). That was precisely the reason she was attracted to him.

Meanwhile, my initial efforts to convince Vita to practice had been doomed to failure because, as the Pacific High School student had tried to explain to her gardening teacher, "You should do the thing you're teaching." All along I had been right that it takes discipline and practice in order to play Bach well. Yet despite the fact that it wasn't long before Ishmael actually performed one of the Beethoven cello sonatas — with a different cellist — and Vita soared way beyond John and the rest of us when we played the Mozart piano quartets, it had been John who had led Vita, far more directly than her piano teacher or I could have, to Bach.

Although she had wanted to learn how to play the piano and had said outright that she wanted to play the Bach minuets "like Ishmael," there was no way at four and a half that she could conceive of what that meant. As she said herself once, "Do you remember when you first asked me if I'd like to take piano lessons? You were trying to make the bed while I jumped on it, and when you asked me, I said 'sure.' But you know, the funny part is that I had *no* idea how totally piano lessons would change my life." Neither had I.

As with math, my conception of what music was had been so limited that I inadvertently made Vita's practicing and those minuets my goal, threatening to limit, by my own limitations, her ability to explore and make real sense of the musical culture she hoped to enter into. If I overstepped my bounds with Vita, though, it was *not* because of my unbridled enthusiasm, as John showed me when he unleashed his on Vita, but because music wasn't properly my work to invite her to share in the first place.

It was John, meanwhile, who could rightly introduce her to musical culture in all its variety and show her what music could be, simply because he was so much a part of it. Thanks to John and his love of music, Vita was able to embrace musical culture, knowing, long before I did, that there is no *one* musical culture, no one right way to play music. Long before I did, she knew, too that although John had very little patience for what musicians normally think of as disciplined musical work — scale exercises and etudes, for example — he was serious about music. She knew that when he said, "Ah, how like Horowitz," he was telling her that she too was a serious musician. Eventually, as a serious musician, she decided to play Bach. She could make that decision because she was now knowledgeable and capable enough to make that *her* goal.

Later, although Vita continued to love experimenting with John, she turned to other musicians as her models, using them, as she had John, as materials with which to gain deeper insight into music and further access into the musical world. Ishmael has been, and will perhaps always be, the most important musician in her life, as "resident composer and keyboard artist" at The Irving Place Conservatory (and as winner, I should add, of almost every prize that the institution has awarded!). There have been other performers and players in Vita's life, as well, and even formal teachers, although they haven't been easy to find.

"When I started studying with Michael," Vita used to tell people, "I had already had three piano teachers, and I was barely eight."

What she didn't say was that they had all tried to teach her how to read music and had failed. But Michael Salmirs, perhaps because he *was* a pianist, and had very little sense of what it meant to be a teacher, never tried. At Vita's first lesson he simply handed her the first movement of a Beethoven sonata and set of Schumann pieces and said, "See if you can learn these by next week." She did.

At the next lesson, he never asked her how many hours she had practiced, but instead treated her like a fellow musician and went right to work on musical fine points. Then he sent her home with more music to learn, all of it great. She has been studying with him ever since.

Ishmael, perhaps because he had developed such firm ideas about music before he ever had a lesson, was seldom thrown off course by teachers, or by my expectations, the way Vita was. Instead, he used the teachers I found for him when he could, and simply ignored them when he couldn't. Sometimes teachers found him hopeless, and said so.

The teacher Ishmael works with now, though, is, like Carl St. Clair, a working musician with very definite ideas. And yet, as with St. Clair, the whole question of boundaries is meaningless.

"Which movement do you want to start out with?" Phiroze Mehta asks. "Or shall we just go through the whole sonata?" They are working on Brahms' third and last sonata.

Ishmael opens up the music to the right page, and then Phiroze says thoughtfully, "You know, this piece bores me when I listen to it. I don't know why, because when I play it, I get totally caught up in it."

Now Ishmael points to the music. "I've been trying to figure out how to catch this whole chord with the pedal. But then how do I clear the A?"

"Well," Phiroze leans over Ishmael and looks at the music. Then he sits down at his piano, taps his fingers on his leg, and says, "There'll be a slight blur, but you know the ear has to be sensitive enough to filter it out."

Ishmael plays. All the while, Phiroze conducts, sings, plays along, or sits at his piano, silently checking fingerings. "You're playing too soft for Brahms! Bring out that melody. Yes, that's nice! Whoops, both hands important here. No sudden surge. No, it's still coming out more than the others. I'd like to hear more of this. That's it. That's better! Yom bom bom ti bom. Now more! Ti bom bom ti. Sound! Not so soft! 1 and 2 and 3. Now take your time. That's good! Now move it along! Di da da dim — yes, that way! Now expand. Really strong tone. A full forte. Bim rum pum pum pah. Don't rush that! Now a little freedom. Ti dom di. Grow a little bit! Ti da da. Tension! O.K., let's go through this page again. You have to give it a little freedom. Don't be stodgy. Imagine Brahms improvising each section. Boom bim bom bom. Yes!"

Phiroze Mehta's studio is in the basement of the Ithaca College music building. It is a long, narrow room and very ugly — concrete block walls painted a greenish yellow, an old worn carpet, and except for a black and white poster of the pianist, Arturo Benedetti Michelangeli, empty of ornamentation. Sometimes I go with Ishmael to his piano lessons. I sit near the door, at one end of the room, and watch Ishmael play on the far Steinway grand — there are two, side by side — under the narrow window at the top of the wall.

To me, the room always seems prison-like as I enter it since, except for a little strip of sky and bush — the view from the window — the whole world is shut out. Often, as I wait for Ishmael to play, I worry that Phiroze may squash Ishmael's creative spirit by being too directive — by having such definitive ideas about how the music ought to be played. But as Ishmael puts his hands to the keys, I know that with Phiroze, it could never happen.

Phiroze begins to sing, "Da di da da dim da da di bom bom bom," standing by Ishmael's shoulder and conducting, sometimes with one hand, sometimes with two, and suddenly, for me, anyway, the room is transformed. Instead of shutting out the world, it now seems to open up *into* the world, or rather, many worlds, since together, Ishmael and Phiroze create a new world with every new piece they work on. As musical colleagues, they feed off each other's creativity, despite the vast difference in their ages and musical experience. So much like John and Vita.

"What I'd like to do next is write a piece for two pianos," Ishmael tells me. "Did you hear how rich the Brahms sounded when Mr. Mehta played it with me? But what I really need to do is to try to produce that same richness of sound — that same volume of sound and resonance — by myself."

Ishmael hardly says a word at lessons, and yet afterwards, as we walk up the stairs and out to the car, and drive down one steep hill and up another to our house, he just can't keep quiet. "Did you hear what Mr. Mehta said about that book of interviews with Messiaen that he read?"

I nod yes, but Ishmael tells me again anyway.

"Phiroze said that when the interviewer asked Messiaen how he felt about the students who rebelled against his teaching — he taught Boulez and Stockhausen, you know— Messiaen said, 'These students who were absolutely wild and wouldn't follow any of my advice — they were the dearest to me.' Isn't that great?!"

I nod again, "Yes, yes."

CHAPTER

Choosing Friendships

Things are going surprisingly well. I've only been homesick once, and that was when I thought, "Oh no, I won't have Vita to talk to every morning when I brush my teeth." — Ishmael, writing home from a music festival in Vermont

Homeschooling parents often tell me, "You're lucky. Your kids just naturally like reading and writing and all the stuff that the schools think is important."

It's true. Perhaps the reason we have had as much courage as we've had to let Vita and Ishmael develop their own idiosyncratic ways of working and learning is that even when they seem to be the most aimless and unproductive — Ishmael writing opening paragraphs for stories day after day and then tearing them up, or Vita lying on her bed on gorgeous spring afternoons reading *Little Women* and then *Little Men* and then *Little Women* all over again — we know that they are still keeping up, academically, with children in school. What they love to do most is precisely what the schools, at least in theory, value most. Not that Vita and Ishmael ever seemed to care, or even to notice. To Ishmael, for example, a day was a day was a day:

April 30: I read *The Rose and the Ring*, by Thackery.

May Day: Wrote a letter to Grandpop. I read part of *From the Earth to the Moon* by Jules Verne. We went to a co-op and got lots of goodies. It was boring. I am Ishmael. Hurrah! We went on a walk and had a celebration for the finishing of my fort. We worked in the fields and I wrote two poems, one about a knight. The celebration was very nice.

May 2: Me and Vita went on a walk. We saw a mouse hole. Yesterday I finished *From the Earth to the Moon*. Spring is wonderful. Me and Vita did a play. She wrote it. We had a bath and did lots of frolicking, which involved a mix-up of names. I wrote a story about knights which had poetry in it. I also wrote a play called *A Debate of Parliament*. Hurrah! Hurrah for today!

May 5: Vita wrote a little in the book she got for her birthday. I wrote a poem:

Spring is pouring forth its shoots,
Ah, there are so many roots!
I cannot see a single bee.
No fly is buzzing after me.
There may not be so many bees,
But there are very many trees.
Daffodil is yellow.

What a jolly fellow!
Rhododendron is green;
Here only one is seen.
                    — Ishmael's journal, age 8

Vita and Ishmael have never really put us to the test. Ishmael always wrote more than enough to keep the school district happy, even in his dry periods, when carpentry or music preoccupied him. If he was behind in math, his school experience was so much to blame that pleasing the school authorities was the last thing on my mind. Vita, as I said, burst out reading at six and a half, just in time to meet my deadline, and if she couldn't spell, as least I knew that she wasn't alone — hardly a school child I knew could at her age.

Occasionally, Ishmael and Vita *have* felt unpleasant social pressures because their timetables for learning were so out of the ordinary. Ishmael, I remember, was not too happy when, on a long car ride, his grandmother thought it might be fun to recite the multiplication tables. And eight-year-old Vita hated to translate German sentences into English in front of the after-school German class she had joined with Ishmael because she was sure her spelling ought to be better. These were relatively minor problems, though, compared to what some homeschoolers feel when they don't learn "on schedule."

"It used to bother me and still does sometimes," fourteen-year-old Anita Giesy wrote in *Growing Without Schooling*, explaining that she didn't learn how to read until she was twelve. And going on to describe how she felt joining 4-H, knowing that she would be expected to fill out several forms, she said, "I don't think I would have had the guts to do it if my best friend hadn't joined with me. I think I would have chickened out."

No, we have never been put to the test, and because we've mostly dealt with sympathetic (or apathetic) school authorities, we've never had to make a special effort to defend our approach to Vita and Ishmael's education. Only with "socialization" have we never dared candor, and not just with the school authorities but with the media ("Oh yes, Vita and Ishmael have lots of friends. We live in a city neighborhood right across the street from a park...."), friends, relatives, and even the family doctor. Is this because Vita and Ishmael have seemed to us so out-of-step, socially, that we weren't even sure in our own minds if what we were doing was defensible?

Just recently, at Vita's first office visit after another ordeal in the hospital, the doctor, worried that she was depressed and still traumatized by the experience, asked, "Has Vita been out playing with her girl friends and socializing much?"

"Translate that 'ladies on the block and music teachers,'" I told myself, as if to convince even myself that her dear friends down the street who invite her over to bake cookies or come over here for formal doll tea parties, and her piano and violin teachers, Michael and Roberta, who adore cats and could play all day with our sixteen-pound fuzzball, Tolly, are "as good as" girl friends.

"No, she hasn't been out much," I admitted, feeling as worried as the doctor was.

Two weeks later, at our next visit, though, I was happy to be able to report, "I really think Vita's fine. She's been eating well, working on art projects, and playing music again. And she's been spending a lot more time with her friends."

"Yeah," Vita eyed me knowingly, as if to say, "playing with Michael and Roberta's cats and having that fun time with Mrs. Mineka, looking at her daughter's old dolls and eating strawberry tarts."

Even more than the ways in which Vita and Ishmael have gone about learning music, writing, or math, the way they have pursued their social lives has often seemed to break such new ground that with no one else's experience to fall back on, we have felt confused, worried, and just plain insecure. We could never see far enough ahead to be able to assure ourselves that Vita and Ishmael would turn out all right. We had no scale against which to measure them, as we had with their reading and math. All we could do was look at them from day to day to assure ourselves that they were happy, and yet often I didn't know whether to laugh or cry at what I saw. "The snow has been melting," Ishmael wrote:

> Ishmael discovered FIVE things.
> FIVE things: 1. rock (huge)
> 2. ledge
> 3. grass
> 4. rock
> 5. blueberry bushes
> First Ishmael discovered crocuses.
> Second Ishmael discovered daffodils.
> Third Ishmael discovered a flower which he didn't know what it

was.

Then came tulips.

Ishmael found a friend.

He made a sale.

He also made a boat.

The friend was named Dana. Dana was nice.

It is spring and Ishmael knows that he has never been so happy.

— Ishmael's journal, age 6

I now think it was *my* insecurity, more than anything, that upset me so much when, during the first couple of months after we took Ishmael out of school, our superintendent returned our proposed curriculum with the comment that, among other things, it was incomplete because we had failed to address our "specific objectives" and "long-range goals" for socialization, one of the district's required "units of study."

"Who are they kidding?" I fumed. "Ishmael's social life is none of their business! There's *no way* we're going to study it. What do they think I'm going to do, assign him lessons and homework in socialization?"

In the end we simply left that item out of our curriculum. The school district never bothered us about it. Ishmael, meanwhile, kept himself busy, oblivious to the whole notion of socialization.

Actually, Ishmael's social life had been a concern of ours long before the question of homeschooling even came up, perhaps because it is the one area in which parents are expected to take an active role from the beginning. We felt responsible for integrating Ishmael socially — teaching him to share and so on — in a way that we never felt responsible for his reading or other academic work. Time and time again we went out of our way to do what we thought would be best for him.

When Ishmael was just eighteen months old, for example, we were convinced that he needed friends, and so we drove him forty-five minutes each way over rutted Vermont roads to a "very nice" nursery school. What happened there was pretty funny, actually, and even we had to laugh. As if to spite us, he headed straight for the carpentry corner and spent all his time hammering and sawing. The vise fascinated him, but he didn't relate to a single kid.

Not about to give up, I began seeking out other two year olds, almost indiscriminately, and invited them over to our house. Ishmael noticed them only long enough to make it clear that my attitude toward sharing was not his. "Mine," he growled frantically, as he grabbed his toys away from his little friends. Often, while I took a book to bed to recover from those all-too-frequent episodes, Ishmael skipped up the stairs to the neighbors', distracting them mercilessly from their work with his stories and acrobatics. But they were grown-ups, and in my eyes, anyway, didn't serve the same kind of crucial social function as other kids.

When we moved to rural New Hampshire, one of the things that immediately attracted us to the town was the small red school building. Bob and I had both gone to schools in affluent, suburban communities, and somehow, as we grew older, we felt cheated, as if our schooling had kept us separate from and ignorant of a whole segment of American reality.

If Vita and Ishmael went to this tiny rural school, we told ourselves, with the children of farmers, factory workers, small tradespeople, and the unemployed, they would grow up with a greater sympathy and understanding than we had ever had for the hardships and rugged determination of this nearly invisible backbone of American society. It was important for them to mingle with other children, we thought, but it was even more important for them to mingle with *these* children.

Our idealist visions aside, though, the idea of teaching Vita and Ishmael ourselves never even occurred to us as a serious option, then, because we were convinced that they needed to work and play with other children outside the narrow confines of our home and family. Home, we thought, should be the warm loving place for children to return to, but not the place for them to learn how to function in society. For better or for worse, we figured, children need to experience the "real world."

By the beginning of Ishmael's second year in school, though, we realized that even if there *were* social benefits to be derived from going to school, Ishmael was not going to be able to take advantage of them. He was far too miserable. He was so miserable, in fact, that there was no longer any question of keeping him in school at all. For us, the challenge would now be, "How do we find comparable social experiences for Ishmael outside of school?"

"It's just a matter of making the extra effort," we assured our friends, relatives, school authorities, and particularly, ourselves. "You know," we explained, "Ishmael will just have to go out and make friends. After all, that's what we do, right? It's not as if we have the luxury of being thrown together for six hours a day with thirty people of exactly our own ages."

If anything, though, it was Bob and me who made the effort. We arranged to send Ishmael to after-school art and drama classes in town, we drove him to piano, pottery, and French lessons with other teachers, and we helped to organize weekly get-togethers with three other homeschoolers and their families.

Ishmael, meanwhile, was quietly building a social life of his own. It wasn't organized, though, it wasn't like school in any way, and so we either discounted it or never even noticed it, I'm not sure which.

> Sept. 1: Began *Smokey*. Then I had a piano lesson. Me and Vita built a town and had a war in it with cannons (weights) and cannonballs (marbles).
>
> We worked on the pond for awhile. It flooded during the night, but my canal was working well, for once. We already have built most of the dam.
>
> Then I went up and played checkers with Vita.
>
> We had lunch and we finished the checker game and did a chess game. I won.
>
> I went to the Edes' and Winterholers' looking for news. They weren't at home. Then I went home and typed all the news I had into a newspaper. I had gotten most of the news yesterday. Next Nancy typed three poems for me.
>
> I helped Vita build her house walls and then we went to the Durhams' and Mouls', selling newspapers. Then I wrote in my diary, did accounts and helped Vita begin a newspaper of her own. Finally we had supper. Next we went to the Dickermans' and got some milk. We watched the geese. — Ishmael's journal, age 8

To the school board, we made every attempt to put Ishmael's social life in what we thought was a positive light. "We have found that he plays best in small groups," we wrote in our first end-of-the-year report, "where he feels he has a chance to get to know individuals. He has become very close to an extremely bright and active eight-year-old boy, and they see each other every Wednesday to do special projects together and, most important, to play."

We also submitted a letter from Ishmael's pottery teacher. "I have found Ishmael to be an excellent balance of serious student and playful child. We have serious talks together. We make jokes. He has an outstanding sense of humor. He is equally at home climbing a tree (which he loves to do) or taking instruction."

We did our best to impress the school authorities with these reports — the authorities had the power, after all, to send Ishmael back to school. Yet it wasn't as if we, too, didn't feel that while it was all well and good for Ishmael to be reading and writing at supposedly precocious levels, he needed to have fun as well. Fun to us meant just what it did to the school board — trees to climb, clay to mess around with, and needless to say, other children. We read and reread the pottery teacher's letter to the school board. Ah yes, we repeated as if to reassure ourselves, "balance." Despite everything, he finds Ishmael to be "an excellent balance of serious student and playful child." Whew!

We had sent Ishmael to first grade with visions of sugar plums dancing in our heads. Not forgetting our own school experiences, but sure that this school would be different, we had delicious images of children working together on science projects and school plays, reading happily in the library, and raising grass snakes in terrariums. We imagined the playground — Ishmael sledding down hills with friends; Ishmael rolling around the fields in the great big truck tires that some parent had donated to the school; Ishmael sitting on top of the jungle gym with that one best friend he could tell everything to. Now, when none of that had worked out, we felt responsible for reproducing it all at home.

Continually, though, one thing after another went wrong. The get-togethers with the other homeschoolers petered out. Ishmael liked his after-school classes well enough, but he didn't make any new friends ("We're here to work, not talk," one of the teachers said), and between school, snow drifts, and bitter cold weather, there were long stretches when Ishmael didn't see the neighborhood kids.

Although we had by then learned to take Vita and Ishmael's play seriously enough not to interrupt or disturb it consciously, we had not yet adequately learned the extent to which, for them, the whole notion of distinguishing work from play, fantasy from reality, seemed absurd. We didn't adequately understand that the idea of "balance" had no relevance to their lives, or that all along — from the moment Ishmael had headed for the vise in the nursery school — they had taken full responsibility for shaping their own so-called social lives, and fully expected to. What often seemed to me to be haphazard and disorganized was, in fact, perfectly balanced, if only because for Vita and Ishmael balance was never an issue.

When a local author of children's books advised nine-year-old Ishmael to "write about what you know," Ishmael came to me and said, "Isn't that what I *have* been doing? I know all about sea adventures and buried treasure and pirates from exploring the brook and rafting in the pond, and from reading *Kidnapped* and *Treasure Island*."

"Yes," I thought, "as well as or better than you know about breakfast from eating it," thinking of all the times Ishmael had come into breakfast, so preoccupied with a story he was writing that I was sure he didn't know whether he was eating French toast or oatmeal. Like me, who wrote about Vita and Ishmael in my journal because the act of writing about them brought them into sharper focus for me, so the act of writing fantasy made the fantasy more real to Ishmael — more immediate, certainly, than the oatmeal sitting before him.

During these early years, Ishmael was obsessed by his two fictional characters, Tom and Mickey. They led lives of high adventure, which Ishmael couldn't let go of, even in his own life, even during the serious business of his school day. Mickey took to danger and intrigue like a fish to water:

> Mickey rafted down the canyon and then past his house and finally into another river. He traveled on and finally came around a bend and saw the sea, There were a few ships there. He had an idea. "I will hide in a ship, and it will go to another country, and I will live there, and will not have to pay to get there." He climbed up a tree and waited for dark. Soon it was night time. Quickly he slipped on board, crawled into a barrel full of wheat and pulled in a clay bowl and some matches from his bag, which he hid. After a while, he fell asleep. When he woke up, it was midnight. He got out of his barrel, and cooked pork over a fire in his clay pot. Then he ate it, put out the fire, and got back into the barrel with everything else. Finally he fell asleep.

To Ishmael, life seemed no less tame. In a typical journal entry he wrote:

> Oct. 4: I am determined to dig a cave and make an island. I know of about three islands, two of which, next spring, will never be there again, for next year they will build a lake covering half a mile of delightful land. I hope that I will be able to sail across it, to find adventures. I also hope that there will be a few islands in the middle of the new lake.

Every day Ishmael wove work and play, fantasy and reality together:

> Oct. 18: We had lunch and I sword fought with Vita in the attic. We had the dolls have a circus come along. We played around in the attic and found Nancy's old collection of foreign coins. Finally me and Bob and Vita played chess. I lost.
>
> We had supper and did some performances. I of whistling, Vita of gymnastics, and Nancy and Vita on piano.
>
> Oct. 19: Had breakfast. Then we began cleaning the stove, the stovepipe and the chimney. I had a piano lesson and wrote some maps for a war me and Vita are carrying on. I told Vita and she said that we'd stopped it. I declared war about that. She said she wouldn't fight. Next we played with the dolls, who began a business with stores and had the winter come. I did archery.
>
> Me and Vita played tic-tac-toe and we had lunch. Bob began struggling with trills on the recorder. Me and Vita began washing the dishes, and I had four little people float around on a platter.
>
> Oct. 20: After breakfast I made the dowels into arrows. I then wrote a letter to Grandma Helen. I did some French. Today is Halloween for the dolls, and they went trick-or-treating in the daytime. However they'll have a Halloween party in the evening. They have a jack o' lantern made of a quince. Finally, after a while, I had a piano lesson and did some archery.
>
> — Ishmael's journal, age 9

Work and play, fantasy and reality, younger and older friends — Ishmael apparently made no distinctions. He never gave a thought to the ages of his friends. He played with the babies and toddlers in the neighborhood as readily as the children his own age I found for him, and it seemed only normal to him to have close relationships with adults (including Bob and me). Friends were friends. Perhaps it was because of this attitude, too, that he often seemed just as happy doing things by himself as with other people. He included himself among his good friends. And why not?

> March 29: I wrote an operetta, "Vagabonds," with a quartet, a quintet, and trio plus quintet. I did a piano lesson. A wonderful day. It is very warm. I finished the *Doughnut Drop-out*, which is very funny. I played dolls. I'm out of practice. I had lunch and played boats in a mud puddle with a box and some wine bottles. I read *The Diary of a Goose Girl*.

Not very good.

— Ishmael's journal, age 9

In the summer months Ishmael and Vita played with the neighborhood kids, but the level of play was often so high-pitched and chaotic that it exhausted both them and me.

As with all kids, I suppose, bikes were the big thing. "I remember this one time," Vita reminded me recently, "when Amy and Kurty came over and we rode up and down the road until we came to that big mossy rock. Then Kurty told Amy to guard us and not let us get away. But we decided to get away. We sort of dashed for it, only on our bikes. Amy came running after us and called for Kurty so that he could help her. Ishmael said that he was going to go around through the woods so that he could ambush Kurty. So I was riding really fast, but then I looked back to see if Amy was close at my heels. There was a big stone right in the middle of the road, but I didn't see it. The bike fell over and of course I fell off the bike. I bruised all my fingers and I ran home crying. Amy felt sorry for me and didn't continue the fight, but I always blamed Ishmael for deserting me."

Ishmael, joining Vita in reminiscing, told me, once again, of the seemingly inevitable warfare that plagued our back field. "This is something that I'm really ashamed about. Kim Nash and Vita and I wanted to have a war with Kurty and Amy. We were very enthusiastic. It never occurred to us that we could be on the same side as them. They weren't interested, but we collected the little seed pods that grew in the big patch of bamboo — you know, to throw at each other. We collected a whole lot, but since they didn't really want to have a battle, they didn't bother. Then we set up a battle plan. Kim set it up so that we had a barricade to hide behind. We'd step forward and throw the pods at Kurty and Amy and they'd throw them back. That wasn't particularly interesting and so fairly soon Kurty got tired of it all and, well, I think he threw a rock and hit me in the eye, but maybe it was just a seed pod and I hadn't realized how hard they were. Then we felt *really* aggrieved. About that time you came over and so the first thing that I did was to go up to you and complain that Kurty had thrown a rock at me. Well, then we forgot the war and went and made tunnels through the bamboo."

Perhaps what was ultimately so exhausting for Vita and Ishmael, although I couldn't have put it into words then, was the way the chaos drove a wedge between their work and their fantasy play — that is, because of the chaos, their play could no longer remain serious.

July 30: ...Shawn Grace, Kim, Abby, and Crystal came over and we did a play. It was another play, lengthened and changed. It all got confused and Nancy had to interfere and direct us, but finally we did a good job. Shawn left. Then we tried to pick blueberries at Green Ledges, but the people were there.

Then we played at the rope swing and Crystal began wondering how long it was till supper. Kim began trying to force me to build a club house. Finally we decided to make it in the shed. After a while me and Crystal went up the Nash-Grace residence to find out if it was supper-time. We found out that, by the Nash clock, it was twenty minutes to five o'clock.

Then I went home, but Kim and Abby didn't go home until after a while. I found out that it was really an hour to five. Then Kim and Abby came back.

We voted Kim chairman of the Newspaper Club. Then we paid taxes to the treasury box and had a meeting.

After a while they went home and we had supper. I woke up in the middle of the night and couldn't get back to sleep

July 31: I had a piano lesson. Vita learned to ride her bike uphill for quite a way. Then I wrote two chapters of a story I'm making about some people who were outlawed by the CIA for demonstrating. After a while I had a fight with Vita on the porch. I played blocks with her. Then we had lunch and Kim, Abby, Crystal and Shawn came over.

We did the play very sloppily, because no one concentrated. Shawn played the piano while in the backstage, and was too late to stab me. After a while we had a meeting and elected Shawn to be chairman. We quickly began fighting over taxes and some other things.

Bob and Nancy cut down a hemlock tree in front of the house. Then Crystal said that she wanted to choose a new chairman. Kim began to grumble at the shortness of her term and finally walked out of the house.

After a while we picked blueberries and Nancy sent them home. A dog wandered into the house and we drove him home.

Aug 1: We went to the Nash-Grace residence to see their dog, Nicky, have puppies. She had thirteen, but three died and she ate one. Then we went home, had our piano lessons at the same time, and went up there again. We told Mary Ann, who, I think, is Kim's mother, that we would perform the play at seven o'clock.

Kim, Abby, and Crystal came over to rehearse the play, but then we realized that Shawn wasn't there, so we couldn't do it...

Ishmael's journal, age 9

Ishmael doesn't say so, but days like this drove him (and often Vita, too) into near hysterics. His plays, and even his club rules and protocol, with their elections and taxes, were far more important to him than just play. Yet with so many kids running around, arguing over parts, changing lines, knocking down scenery, and not showing up for rehearsals or performances, there was no way he could hope to maintain any kind of day-to-day continuity or organization. Increasingly, Ishmael and Vita preferred to play with each other or to hang around with Bob and me.

"I remember when we were planting the blueberries in front of the house," Vita told me years later, "and you saw Billy coming along down the road. You said, 'Would you like to play with Billy?' and I said I'd rather not. So you said, 'Then run around to the back of the house where Bob is working,' and so I did. He was cutting up the old elm tree. You told Billy that I was working and couldn't play."

Each fall, with no other playmates to "wreak havoc," as Ishmael once put it, they went back to their doll games, serious theater, and music with obvious relief:

Oct. 1: I found out how the sound of a note on the piano usually resembles the sound of a note on any other instrument, so if you maybe wanted to write a string quartet or whatever, you just have to write a piano piece in the range of your instruments.

Then I copied the notes of a certain piano exercise in different keys. I also practiced a little bit and we drove off to a piano lesson...

Later I chopped down some pumpkins from their stalks and then I chopped down a lot of old corn stalks and chopped down some asparagus which I didn't know was still alive and growing...

Oct. 5: The Queen of Dolls asked a subordinate queen to be a duchess so the real queen could get all the tax money needed instead of the other queen getting some of the money from the Queen's land. The subordinate queen raised a revolt, and was outlawed. Then the real queen's friend turned up!

I had a piano lesson and me and Nancy found out that "Arkansas Traveller" was written for two pianos and that the only reason our hands hadn't run into each other was that I had been playing an octave too high.

Me and Vita had lunch and we went on a long, long hike. We sword fought with grass and juggled apples...

Oct. 10: Had breakfast. I kept copying my Mozart report into script. I also did some math. We played dolls a lot and I did some division and

French. I wrote a letter to Bardy and Grandpop and we had lunch.

Me and Vita gave a surprise concert with our instruments that we had kept secret and we arranged to partly put the play "Moneybags" to music with them. We did a rehearsal with Nancy watching. She switched the story of "Moneybags" around a little, so it would be more understandable. We did "Moneybags," "Abdul the Bulbul Ameer," "The Burnt Cakes," and "The One Runaway."

I wrote down the new version of "Moneybags," had a piano lesson, and me and Vita chased each other a lot. Then we listened to the record of "Peter and the Wolf," by Prokofiev. Bob and Vita went for milk at the Dickermans' and I listened to Haydn's "Toy Symphony."

We had supper, the Doll Constitution was finished and then we played around with codes.

— Ishmael's journal, age 9

Although the frantic summertime play wore me out equally, I never quite shared in Ishmael's and Vita's relief when the neighborhood kids went back to school and to huddling around their winter fires. I still thought of them as a gift — whether a welcome gift or not seemed almost irrelevant. The main thing was that for eight long months Vita and Ishmael would have no choice but to play by themselves. When I saw them turn to our friends, joining in our conversations and activities, I thought of it as just a poor substitute.

Still, Ishmael seemed happy sitting on the porch with Bob and our friend from up the road, talking about poetry and philosophy. When Bob's old friend, Graham, stayed for several months, Ishmael always hung around after supper listening to him talk about books and music.

As Vita once wrote about that visit, "I remember sitting with Graham on the porch and looking at the beautiful view with the goldenrod and the stream and the weeping willow. Graham was painting it like he saw it and I was feeling very important and pretending that I was too. But I had never tried to paint what I saw and so really, I was just fooling around. Of course, our pictures were not at all alike."

Because we lived in rural New Hampshire, where neighbors were few and far between but weekend and summer visitors plentiful, many of Vita's and Ishmael's relationships with adults were primarily long-distance. They wrote lots of letters and were thrilled when they received them:

Dear Vita,

I have just finished reading *Bored*, by Vita Wallace, and my first feeling after it ended was, "Oh, too bad!" I enjoyed it so much I wanted to go on reading it. The story about the bicycle was my favorite because it showed you are a real writer: have an unfortunate experience and make it into a story! But I like the others very much, too. And I'm glad you took the little mouse back to his hold.... Love, Grandma

Dear Vita,

That is a pretty nice cathedral you made, or at least the picture you drew of it looks good.

Do you know that there are a number of nuts in the world who will play golf in any kind of weather, and almost day or night? So you have to be particularly careful about skiing on golf courses. It's almost as bad as skiing in traffic; and which would you rather be hit by, a golf ball or a Volkswagon?

I'm glad that you and Ishmael are creating daily compositions. Practice, they say, makes perfect, and about the time you are eight you should be doing some fine things. Do you enjoy writing the words or the music better? Love, Benji

Dear Ishmael,

You all would laugh at the scene in my office. Steve Rupprecht, who just started working with us (and is a good guitar player, a real pro), has just started for the first time to play the violin, and he's having a ball, doing all the things I like, trying stuff out, doing trills, double stops, and getting a nice small sound from the instrument. Beside him on the couch is Dannette Finn (5), playing a pianica, and also doing some fine improvising. So I have a kind of modern-sounding duet....

Steve is doing trills, spiccato bowing, octaves — the works! Now a glissando way up to the high positions! I'm going to try to persuade him to keep playing the violin. He likes it and seems to have a lot of talent for it. Of course, he is already a very skilled musician, which makes a difference....

As always, I envy you guys, having so much time for music. Wish I could be around more to hear more of what you're doing. I guess you're having a wonderful time. I've been playing my cello quite a bit the past three or four days, and as a result it is sounding better. But if it doesn't get a lot of work every day it gets a bit hard and dry.... Was thinking the other day about a composer's style — the advantage of having a developed style is that you can write music without having to think about every note; the danger is that soon you can write music without thinking about any note, just turn on the style machine and let it run. Happens a lot to composers. Love, John

Vita's and Ishmael's interests, ways of thinking and going about their own activities, and even their language began to reflect these relationships. During Vita's last hospital stay we heard one of the surgeons, explaining her case to another doctor out in the hall, say, "The kid's a prodigy-type. You know, you can almost talk to her like an adult."

Blood flowing into a vein in one arm, sugar water flowing into a vein in the other, and a tube running up her nose and down into her stomach, she whispered to me furiously, "How would he know? He's never bothered to try." And then, sitting up in bed, she added, "Put what he said into your book!"

Well, Vita, here it is. I knew without her having to say another word that, as far as she was concerned, the doctor had been doubly insulting. Not only did she think he was calling her names ("I am *not* a 'prodigy-type'!"), but she had always taken it for granted that anyone who bothered *could* talk to her "like an adult" ("You know, like a person"). After all, many of her closest friends *were* adults!

"Rolfe called just to talk," Vita wrote in her diary, about her former violin teacher, "and it ended up that he came over at 12:30. (I'm usually not done practicing by then, and so I had to hurry, hurry, hurry.) As I suppose I should have guessed, he does almost all the second movement of the Mendelssohn on the D string!"

In another entry she wrote, "Today I went with C.R. Fellman — Carolyn Rose Fellman, I mean — to Susan Andrews' house. She is a doll-maker. Her house is filled with dolls. She makes wood, cloth, paper, and clay dolls! There is hardly anything in the house that doesn't have a doll sitting on it."

Despite the pleasure that friendships like these gave Vita and Ishmael (and despite my disdain for the doctor), there was still no way that they could even begin to fit my lingering image of healthy childhood friendships. Certainly they didn't come close to substituting for "that one best friend" that still preoccupied me.

When Ishmael was ten and Vita almost seven, we moved to Ithaca, New York, to a neighborhood with a park right across the street. As I wrote in *Better Than School*, Bob hung up a tree swing, and suddenly there were kids — kids in the park, kids in the street, kids in the yard, and kids in the house. And neither rain, sleet, nor snow could keep these kids away! Finally, for the first time ever, Vita and Ishmael had the materials they needed — not to build an intellectual structure, perhaps, but certainly to build a social one! Yet what typically happened took me by surprise. The other children came and went, and more than ever, Vita and Ishmael absorbed themselves in their dolls, their private jokes, their newly founded "music conservatory" and simply, their music.

When Vita was nine, or maybe ten, I happened, one afternoon, on Annabel-the-doll's birthday party and was amazed by how many doll friends she had. I said so to Vita, who answered quite matter-of-factly, "Yes, and it isn't any trouble for them to come over, since they all live under the bed together anyway, you know, just like me and Ishmael, only we don't live under the bed, of course."

Sometimes it only takes a few words from a child to finally open our eyes. Vita was right — it wasn't "any trouble" for her to get together with Ishmael. But was that such a bad thing? Until now I had always assumed that they had been forced to be friends by convenience, not choice. But why? Suddenly it became clear to me that when they giggled together in the bathroom and told each other stories, or sang together on walks, they were being just as jovial as Annabel and her friends at the birthday party. What's more, it was that very kind of giggling and singing that I had always imagined when I'd thought longingly about "that one best friend."

And yet Vita and Ishmael's bond was even tighter. Without the usual interruptions imposed by school and parents all pulling them in different directions, summer camps, vacations, and the inevitable turnover of friendships that comes with moves and school graduations, they had been able to bridge the gap between work and play effectively by developing games that could evolve in complexity over a long period of time. The unspoken rules of their games formed a bond that I knew I would probably never begin to comprehend.

Perhaps only siblings, I now realized, could have created a country like Skirmishia, peopled with dolls of all shapes and sizes, each with specific family relationships and functions in the economy. Perhaps only siblings could have invented, and built upon year after year, Skirmishia's elaborate economy, system of government, and complex history of wars and occasional peacetime.

Probably only siblings could have invented a school like The

Irving Place Conservatory, with its schedule of lessons in composition, voice, and theory and formal concerts with invited audiences. All those years, so many wonderful things were happening, and yet I'd barely noticed, simply because my preconceptions about how things ought to be had been so different — siblings *couldn't* be best friends. (Now, if only I could hope to explain all that to the school authorities or Vita's doctor! But I guess it's really just something you have to *see*.)

Now that they've grown older, Vita and Ishmael are branching out, looking for close friendships beyond our immediate family — always in terms of their work, though, never simply in a wild search for other kids. "I think of Aleeza as one of the people in Ithaca I enjoy seeing most." Ishmael once wrote. "The others are Carolyn Fellman, Stephen May, Louise Yavalow and Trudy Borden." Aleeza is a young pianist Vita's age; Carolyn is an artist and theater director (and Vita's good friend as well) who has produced several of Ishmael's operettas; Stephen and Louise taught Ishmael composition and music theory; and Trudy was Ishmael's beloved piano teacher — the first person he ever met who cared about sound the way he did. She was the one, too, who gave him his introduction to contemporary music.

Since then, Ishmael's "list" has expanded considerably, although to many people, he must still appear to be socially isolated. The mother of a friend of Vita's told me recently that I "really ought to see that he has a chance to play music with his age-peers, and not just musicians at his own level, since they always seem to be so much older."

I can't imagine anything drearier for Ishmael. Yet over the past few years he *has* made friends with several young musicians, although their ages have always been purely incidental to their friendship. To one young friend, away in Japan for the summer, he wrote about playing music with her sister Yumi and meeting her brother Ken for the first time:

> Yesterday the Ivy Trio (Vita, Yumi and myself) performed the Mendelssohn Trio, and Vita and I met Ken, both of which events were really exciting. I had a nice last-minute experience on the Mendelssohn: because, as I had always had to work on it separately from the music that I worked on with my teacher, I had not ever had time to work on more than the bare minimum of technical things, and then on the day before I realized that I didn't have a clear mental vision of the piece, so I went with the music out onto the porch swing, where I am sitting

now, writing, and listened to it in my head, and all of a sudden I started to see all the really big phrases that the music was made of, and realized that I had really been getting bogged down in individual chords.

Ken turned my pages at the concert, because I had still not yet gotten myself together to figure out how to deal with them myself. Then at the party afterward he showed me his record collection, which is quite wonderful. He has a lot of really old records of the greatest violinists and pianists, for instance, Kreisler, Dinu Lipatti, and Horowitz, bought for incredibly low prices at Japanese antique shops. He played me part of Horowitz's first recording of the Beethoven "Pathetique" sonata, which was really nice. Then we played a good deal of music together, including the Kreisler that I played with you, and the Vitali Chaconne, which I remember you were going to play — a really great piece.

Ken, Yumi, and Lili, Ishmael's correspondent, are Vita's friends too, but her own particular friends include, first and foremost, the ladies who live down the street, loyal attendees of Conservatory recitals and functions and frequent guests or hostesses at doll tea parties. ("Mommy," Vita asked one day, "Why did Mrs. Stinson say that Harry told her she was crazy to set up the tea things for Rachelle?" Rachelle is the red-haired porcelain doll Vita made for her. "Because Harry probably thought she was too old to be playing with dolls," I said. "But that's *exactly* why I love her," Vita told me.) Both Vita's and Ishmael's friends are, in a very real sense, their colleagues — not just "the kids on the block," but people with whom they share work.

Thinking of this, I have been interested to watch Vita develop three long-distance relationships with girls of approximately her own age. She met them through the pages of *Growing Without Schooling* and continues to know them only through the mail, as pen-pals. She was drawn to them because of things she knew they did well and that she was interested in doing better herself. Heather puts out a newspaper, *Kid News,* and is a masterful typist; Amanda is a writer who not only can write good fiction but can spell; Jamie is an artist who doesn't shy away from drawing people.

As I wrote in GWS #61, "What I find so lovely about Vita's relationships with these three friends is that although they are better than she is at certain skills, she doesn't feel any mean-spirited pressure to compete with them, or any need to catch up. Their example simply shows her what *she* can do if she tries."

Susannah Sheffer responded by asking if I felt that the ages of these friends made any difference to Vita, and suggested that perhaps their work might seem more "accessible" to her, more "easily duplicable" in some ways, than that of older people. I hadn't thought of it like that before, since so often Vita finds adults' work perfectly accessible, but I was immediately reminded of how important Vita and Ishmael have been to each other *as children*.

In GWS #62 I continued the discussion:

> You used the word "accessible" to describe the way Vita might view Amanda's writing. Looking back, I can see just how accessible Vita and Ishmael have made certain ideas, skills, and projects seem to each other in a way that no adult, as a role model, could have. Ishmael, for example, has seen me make banana bread a hundred times, and yet it was only when he saw Vita mashing the bananas that he said, "I'd like to help too." Only after Vita walked to the bagel shop by herself and arrived home safely, a bag of fresh bagels securely in her hand, did he realize that he could go out on his own and buy bagels too.
>
> As you implied, sometimes the adult world seems so impossibly distant to children that it takes children themselves to show other children what is really possible — to help them see that "If she can do it, so can I." Jamie's drawing [for example] showed Vita what she herself was capable of, but after a summer of intense work, she was able to go beyond that initial discovery. Jamie's age was no longer a factor for Vita because drawing, for her, had moved into the realm of serious work. Jamie... is now simply one of Vita's colleagues.

For Bob and me, the fact that Vita and Ishmael have no peer group in the conventional sense — that is, no pressure from peers to act in certain ways or do certain things — but simply their colleagues and each other, has had an interesting and quite unexpected effect on our relationship with them. When Vita chooses to wear what we would normally consider to be outlandish clothes combinations, for example — say, a plaid shirt with a pink flowered skirt — I am never tempted to dismiss her choice with the thought, "Oh no, what kind of a fad is that?", as if she's just "following the crowd" and is incapable of doing any real thinking on her own. She has no crowd to follow, of course, and so I know that she *has* to be thinking for herself. Why, I wonder instead, does she seem to have no sense of conventional aesthetics? Why do I have one? Rather than assuming that Vita has poor taste, I wonder if there *is* such a thing as an absolute aesthetic value, or if, perhaps, my tastes weren't simply formed by what I quickly learned were socially acceptable norms.

When Ishmael puts on a record and sits on the couch, hunched over the album cover and listening to what I can only think of as unrelated sounds, I *may* shut the front door — there are the neighbors to consider — but I never dismiss the music the way my parents did when I listened to Bob Dylan or The Grateful Dead, or even as my friends do now, as their own kids turn away from Bach and back to (I still can't quite believe it) The Grateful Dead again. Ishmael doesn't listen to The Grateful Dead, but rather to Boulez, Stockhausen, and Cage. Yet even if he did, I would assume that he was doing so for a good reason. Knowing that he thinks for himself, just as Vita does, makes me take his choices and ideas seriously. For Vita and Ishmael, knowing that we seriously care what they think and are eager to learn from them has meant that they are still eager to teach us, to talk to us about everything, and to feel close to us in a way that I never thought possible between parents and children.

If we have regrets, now, about their social lives, it is only that they really haven't had many opportunities to get to know people from different backgrounds. Except for a few of our neighbors in New Hampshire, they have seldom played with poor kids, black or other minority kids, or even foreign kids. School, though, we realized early on, was *no* place to do that.

There, we had seen once proud and self-confident children — Ishmael's and Vita's neighborhood friends — become withdrawn and disruptive, ashamed of their parents, who didn't read or "talk right," and embarrassed by their almost immediate academic failure. In school, these kids quickly learned, no one cared about how well you could take a truck engine apart or clean a rifle or babysit your little sister.

School, we realized, would never have been able to bridge the gap between Ishmael and his working-class classmates. Instead, it would almost certainly have created a gap where previously there had been none. School, after all, is where you learn to judge and be judged by narrowly defined academic standards. School is where you learn to stop seeing people "from all vantage points," as Ishmael would say, quoting the Sufi leader, Pir Vilayat Inayat Khan.

Often, because we have had so little to do with the schools over the years, it has been easy for us to forget that. Being reminded is always a shock. A few months ago, for example, Ishmael took the SAT, with the idea that if he did well he could "graduate" early from "The

Wallace Home School" (but *not* The Irving Place Conservatory!), since he's almost sixteen and would then be old enough to "drop out" legally in New York State.

"What a relief," I wrote my father, sending along Ishmael's scores. "He passed."

"He did more than *that*," my father told me confidently, with the weight of thirty-five years of teaching behind him. "Listen, Ishmael's verbal score places him in the top two percent, he's just a bit below average in math, and the score on the standard written English test confirms the verbal score. With scores like that, plus his successes in music, probably even Harvard would find him interesting."

You'd think that my father's words would have made me feel good. It should have been nice to hear that if Ishmael wanted to go to Harvard he might get accepted — not that his ambitions have ever led him anywhere near the contemplation of Harvard's ivy walls, as even my father was quick to point out. But for me, just realizing (as I should have had the imagination to do long ago) that prestigious institutions like Harvard take scores like these seriously, made me cringe. I felt thoroughly disgusted by the idea that it was somehow legitimate to characterize and make judgments about Ishmael based on three numbers.

Of course there is *no way* that those SAT scores could ever reflect Ishmael as we know and love him. "There is no score in the world that could hold or contain Ishmael," I told my father. "No percentile that could ever accurately describe or categorize him. There is simply no way to measure him (or anybody) on any sort of vertical scale. He is too unusual, too complex, and too full of life and wonderment."

And yet I could feel my own weakness. Like most of us I have lived all my life with vertical measurements like SAT scores. Like most of us I have felt good when test scores placed me on top and lousy when they didn't. When my teachers told my mother that I didn't work up to my potential, I was always pleased, imagining "my potential" as an almost unattainable number high up on some scale. "I'm smart after all," I used to think.

Vita and Ishmael, though, seem to have no sense of these vertical scales of comparison that most of us take for granted. They have never measured themselves in any way except against themselves and what they hope to accomplish.

Vita's doctor said to me at our last visit, "Vita is such an intense little girl. I mean, there's got to be a lot of stress in her life, having a brother like Ishmael to live up to."

I appreciated the doctor's wanting to consider the whole of Vita's life as he thought about her medical history, but I wanted to say, "Vita wouldn't even know what you are talking about."

She thinks Ishmael is unquestionably the best musician she knows; she is thrilled every time he has a play produced or wins a prize; and as Director of The Irving Place Conservatory, she has bestowed several prizes on him herself. She adores and admires Ishmael, yet she knows, absolutely, that she has her own life, her own ways of making music, and her own artistic ambitions.

When Ishmael goes downstairs in the morning to practice, he is, in a way, just as nervous as if he were going to play in a piano competition. The important thing, for him, is that he play as well as he can. When he meets new people or thinks of his friends, he would never dream of wondering how well they do in school. He has never thought in terms of "smart" people and "dumb" people as I did in school. Instead, Ishmael sees whole people. He looks for what is interesting in his friends and values them for what he sees — Ken for being such a terrific violinist; Lili for being able to find her way around the streets of Tokyo; Yumi for reading all of Saki ten times over.

By forming friendships with people through what they consider to be their work — their music, their love of theater, books, writing, in Vita's case art, and even dolls — Vita and Ishmael have learned to judge their work and that of others squarely. Yet by judging their friends within the context of their shared work, they have at the same time learned to judge them on their own terms, always appreciating the ways in which their friends have chosen to connect with life. In doing so, they have grown to be some of the most profoundly accepting and caring people I have ever met. At the same time, by doggedly insisting on pursuing friendships within a social structure that feeds their work and doesn't just offer a respite from it, they have managed to protect and to continue to explore and work on what they love most. Of all the good things I hoped for when we took Ishmael out of school, these were ones I could never have imagined or antici-pated. Our undertaking was just too new, and in our experience, unprecedented.

Moving Outward

Exclusive
(for my daughter)

I lie on the beach, watching you
as you lie on the beach, memorizing you
against the time when you will not be with me:
your empurpled lips, swollen in the sun
and smooth as the inner lips of a shell,
your biscuit-gold skin, glazed and
faintly pitted, like the surface of a biscuit;
the serious knotted twine of your hair.
I have loved you instead of anyone else,
every separate grain of your body
building the god, as I built you within me,
a sealed world. What if from your lips
I had learned the love of other lips,
from your starred, gummed lashes the love of
other lashes, and from your shut, quivering
eyes the love of other eyes,
from your body the bodies,
from your life the lives?
Today I see it is there to be learned from you:
to love what I do not own.
                    — from *The Dead and the Living* by Sharon Olds

I never use an electric can-opener if there's an old fashioned hand-operated one anywhere nearby. I only learned how to drive a car so that I could save Ishmael the hour-long bus ride to school. In general, I go out of my way not to drive. I use an old manual typewriter, but far prefer pens and lined paper. For philosophical reasons, I have always been suspicious of gadgets, "labor-saving" devices, and modern technology of any kind.

For one thing, I've noticed that most labor-saving innovations do just the opposite. The invention of the vacuum cleaner didn't make housework any easier for women (nor did it lure men into sharing the work load). Instead, it tempted us into raising our standards for cleanliness. Now we vacuum twice as often as we ever swept, and we expect our floors to be four times as clean. I'm convinced that the mountain of bureaucratic paperwork that we now require of ourselves every time we turn around grows in direct proportion to the availability of computers and word-processors, and to the "miraculous" new programs and software that keep coming out. Wasn't life really much simpler and easier before we invented machines to make life simple and easy?

Strong as my philosophical arguments are, though, the truth is that I've always just had a neurotic aversion to machinery and modern technology. (I grew up with a mother who persisted in calling our G.E. refrigerator an "ice box," which perhaps explains something.) My ideal has always been to live in a log cabin in the middle of the forest, with bird song for music, the full moon for light, and a bubbling brook for running water.

Over the past several years, as has probably happened to everyone, I have lost most of my dear friends to computers and word-processors. These machines are not only addicting, but they bring out a kind of evangelical fervor in people. One after another, my friends advise me to get a computer, and preferably a "Mac." (A Macintosh, for those of you out there who are still uninitiated.) I'd love it, my friends tell me. It would save me untold hours of work, "especially now that you're writing a book," they say. Every time I open one of my notebooks and see how impossibly messy they've become, with cross-outs and revisions, I know my friends are right. Still, I am a hopeless case. I like to write at the kitchen table (or in bed on cold nights). I like the sensual feel of pushing a pen across a pad of paper. It may be slow, but at least it gives me time to think.

When my friends give up on me they turn to Ishmael. I've come to expect it. "The Mac has an incredible new music writing program out — there's no way you should go without it," they tell him. "You'd save so much time it's not funny and of course you'd end up with finished scores that look absolutely professional. I'd think that would be really important if you're serious about competitions. But the other thing is that this program can actually print out the parts. That alone would save hundreds of hours, especially when you go to write that symphony of yours. Even for things like revising it's amazing. You know it can actually play you back what you've just written, blah, blah, blah."

I am convinced that a Mac with music writing program is the way to go for Ishmael and I'd probably even fork over the money, but it has always seemed like such a major investment that I've figured Ishmael should at least show some interest in it before I write the check. So far, he has been politely interested, nothing more. Mostly he's just so busy writing music ("I got an inspiration this morning that I just *have* to write down") that he can't imagine ever finding the time to learn how to use the machine in the first place.

Bob, meanwhile, says that he thinks he could probably use a word-processor, especially now that he too is writing a book, but considering the expense, he'd only want to get one if one of the kids would use it as well. That leaves Vita. "The graphics that you can do on the Mac are really something else! Besides, Vita, of all the Wallaces you're the one with the kind of mind..."

At twelve, Vita still looks to us for approval and guidance and so, although I've certainly never discouraged her from getting involved with computers — I've even encouraged her from time to time — she knows that I am basically an "ice box" sort of person. You can imagine my surprise, then, when, without any hint of embarrassment or subterfuge, she suddenly leapt at the chance to learn how to use one.

This is how it happened: Inspired by Humphrey Berkeley's book, *The Life and Death of Rochester Sneath,* a collection of hysterically funny but absolutely authentic letters pertaining to "Selhurst," the British public school that Berkeley invented, Vita and Ishmael recently made up a mythical music festival, "Broomhaegel Music," and decided to print and post flyers about it to see if they couldn't actually attract some real musicians the way Berkeley attracted prospective parents for his school. ("Then what?" I keep asking, without ever getting a satisfactory answer.) Together, they sketched out the text for the flyer:

> Broomhaegel Music was founded by Mr. and Mrs Ethelred Z. Broomhaegel in 1971, after they had been unable to find a music festival in the USA that lived up to their ideal of a professional but warm and closeknit establishment...

They even included testimonials:

> "I count the summers that I spent at Broomhaegel as the major formative influence in my musical development. I would highly recommend Broomhaegel to any aspiring young artist."
> —Alzebete Hnedy, violinist

In order to make their hoax work, Vita and Ishmael knew that their flyer had to look really good, and so they decided to forget about the transfer letters and xerox machine and go all out with a laser printer. That meant designing the whole thing on a Mac first. Our friend and computer fanatic, Dick Furnas, offered to do the job, but Vita refused. "Then it wouldn't really be ours," she said.

But when Dick suggested a compromise, I wasn't at all prepared for her response. "I'll teach you how to use the Mac," he said, "if you'll help me to revise the mailing lists for the playhouse."

"Great," she said. "When can I start?"

In *GNYS AT WRK,* Glenda L. Bissex's account of how her son learned to read and write, she wrote:

> Except in the form of an individual person's reading a particular text or writing a particular message in a specific situation, reading and writing do not exist. "Reading" and "writing" are abstractions, conven- ient abbreviations enabling us to refer to certain kinds of human activities. Unless we keep reminding ourselves that "reading" and "writing" are abstractions and abbreviations, we may come to believe — or, just as dangerously, to act as though we believed — in their disembodied existence ... [But] we do not read for the sake of reading, nor write for the sake of writing..."Reading" and "writing" are meaning- less as well as disembodied if they are regarded as ends in themselves,

not as means of learning, imagining, communicating, thinking, remembering, and understanding.

Making a similar point about teaching in one of her letters, Susannah Sheffer wrote, "I think teaching should be one of those verbs that *requires* an indirect object to be grammatically correct. It should be impossible to say, 'I was teaching her.' Only sentences like 'I was teaching her writing' should even be open to consideration." Teaching, in the abstract, makes no sense.

Likewise, the idea of using the Mac in the abstract made no sense to Vita. Even when people tried to entice her with its graphics possibilities she wasn't interested. She had too many other art projects on her mind. Yet once she came up with a project for which she knew the Mac would be useful, she was eager to learn how to use it. As Glenda Bissex writes, "Someone reads something *for some purpose.*" Vita only gave the computer the time of day when she had a specific purpose for it in mind.

We think that we need to learn about technology or computers in the abstract, instead of thinking about what in particular we want to do for which computers or other new technology might be helpful. Another idea that we tend to think about in the abstract, instead of as connected to a meaningful purpose, is the idea of "letting go." As a mother, this has been one of the most difficult and frustrating notions I've had to deal with. We are continually advised to "let our children go," as if "letting go" makes perfect sense — as if it's possible and even desirable for children to "go," without having any reason to go or any specific place *to* go. Sometimes it seems as if the pressure starts on day one and just never lets up:

"Please," I had begged in the delivery room. "Let me comfort Ishmael."

"No," the doctor had laughed, as if even then I needed to give Ishmael a chance to be on his own. "He needs to cry. It's good for his lungs."

But it's not just doctors and childhood experts who pressure us. The "letting go" myth is so pervasive these days that even our closest allies often fall for it, making it all the harder for us to trust ourselves and our feelings toward our children.

In her editorial in the Summer 1987 issue of *Mothering,* for example, Peggy McMahon wrote, "With my last child, my tendency has been to do more for her longer than I have done for the other three simply because there has not been a new baby around to remind me of how capable she really is.... We know from observing others that it *is* possible to give too much, to take care of children in ways that disempower them .... We can incapacitate children so that they do not realize their full potential...."

Friends and relatives told me that it would be dangerous for baby Ishmael to sleep in our bed. They told me to stop getting up with him at night after five months ("Before you know it he'll be up frying eggs at midnight") and to wean him at a year ("What are you going to do, nurse him at recess? He'll never wean on his own"). They said, "Send him to nursery school and kindergarten. He needs to spend time away from you." They told me to make him zip his own jacket and learn to tie his shoes. "You can't expect to be his slave for the rest of your life," they said. Could it be true, I wondered, that children will never wean themselves? That they will be content to let other people dress them forever and ever? That they will never want to leave home unless they are pushed out the door?

I was afraid to admit that I missed Ishmael when he was at school. "Vita misses him," I used to say. I didn't tell anyone that I hated to put him on the school bus because there were no seat belts. "I drive him to school because the bus ride is so long," I used to explain, telling only a half-truth. I didn't say that I worried because he got so wet and cold out in the snow at recess and never ate his lunch. (When I wrote about these things in *Better Than School* the editor cut them out. "We wouldn't want to give people the wrong impression," he said.)

When we took Ishmael out of school at the beginning of second grade, the whole issue of "letting go" became something that I couldn't hide from any longer. The school people accused me of being over-protective and the truth is that because I had so little support, I thought they might be right. We sent Ishmael to camp that summer. Did I have to prove to the world, or to myself, that I could cut the apron strings?

The camp was a "non-competitive arts camp," and it boasted of a small theater with organized productions, a pottery studio, several pianos, and a weekly concert put on by the campers. It had the usual lake, hiking trails, and campfires, plus a blueberry patch, organic food, and a few chickens. It sounded great, but the reality was something else. No one greeted Ishmael warmly or helped him get settled in when he arrived — in fact, no one seemed to notice him at all. His bunk counselor was too busy playing his saxophone to do more than say "hi." The pianos were total wrecks, nowhere near in tune, and the organic food looked suspiciously like bologna, white bread, and red popsicles. Still, we convinced ourselves that we had to leave him there, and we did.

In her book, *The Continuum Concept,* which is, in large part, about how the process of "letting go" works in primitive cultures (specifically that of the Yequana Indians of the Venezuelan jungles) and what we can learn from them (plenty), Jean Liedloff writes:

> For some two million years, despite being the same species of animal as ourselves, man was a success. He had evolved from apehood to manhood as a hunter-gatherer with an efficient life style which, had it continued, might have seen him through many a million-year anniversary. As it is, most ecologists agree, his chances of surviving even another century are diminished with each day's activities.
>
> But during the brief few thousand years since he strayed from the way of life to which evolution adapted him, he has not only wreaked havoc upon the natural order of the entire planet, he has also managed to bring into disrepute the highly evolved good sense that guided his behavior throughout all those eons. Much of it has been undermined only recently as the last coverts of our instinctive competence are rooted out and subjected to the uncomprehending gaze of science.

Or, as in my case, the gaze of the school district, the pediatrician, friends, relatives, and especially myself. "Ever more frequently," Jean Liedloff goes on to say, "our innate sense of what is best for us is short-circuited by suspicion while the intellect, which has never known much about our real needs, decides what to do."

I left Ishmael at camp because I was sure I "ought to." He promised to write often, and in fact we later found out that he had, but only two letters got through:

> Dear Nancy, Bob and Vita,
> I am having a good time, but I miss you all a lot. However, I must kick or I will sink.
> Will you please send a pencil? I like them better than pens, and I need to be able to erase in my diary.
> There is a nurse-counselor in camp called Kelly. She sits at our table for breakfast and lunch. I think she has some greedy habits toward ice cream.
> Don't worry. I am fine. Love, Ishmael

P.S. Please send a belt. One time I went to the "Lake House" and I had to put on some long pants. I had to tie them up with rope. Yesterday we went to Sunapee and went to a Craftsman's Fair. I am now in debt one dollar and six cents for a glass of milk. I have been transferred to a bunk above the theater.

Dear Nancy, Bob and Vita,
I was sick but I am fully cured now so don't worry.
The day before yesterday we went on a hike up Mount Sunapee. You can read about it in my diary when I get home.
A friend of mine is planning to go home a while before he is supposed to because he doesn't like camp well enough. I am very sad about this.
I am fine. Love, Ishmael

What Ishmael didn't say, at least in the letters we received, was that he had almost drowned; that he had often gone hungry, especially on over-nights when they routinely ran out of food; and that he never had a chance to work in the theater or play a functioning piano. When we arrived to pick him up he looked ravaged. He was filthy, his hair was crawling with lice, and his face was covered with open sores.

"The human continuum," Jean Liedloff writes, "can be defined as the sequence of experience which corresponds to the expectations and tendencies of the human species in an environment consistent with that in which those expectations and tendencies were formed. It includes appropriate behavior in, and treatment by, other people as part of that environment."

For the baby, born into this natural human continuum,

there are shocks which do not shock, either because they are expected (and would be missed) or because they do not happen all at once. Birth cannot correctly be thought of as marking the baby's completion like the end of an assembly line, for some complements have already been "born" in the womb and others will not become operative until later. Fresh from the series of expectations and their fulfillments in the womb, the newborn infant is expectant, or, more accurately, certain, that his or her next requirements will also be met.

What happens next? Through tens of millions of generations, what happens is the momentous transfer from the entirely alive surroundings inside the mother's body to a partly live one outside it. Though her all-giving body is there, and (ever since the hand-freeing advent of walking erect) her supporting arms as well, there is a great deal of lifeless, alien air touching the infant's body. But he is ready for that too; his place in arms is the expected place, known to his innermost sense as *his* place, and what he experiences while he is in arms is acceptable to his continuum, fulfills his current needs, and contributes correctly to his development.

Jean Liedloff's continuum baby, like that of the Yequana Indians she studied, spends months literally full time in its mother's arms or bundled against her body. It sleeps with her, nuzzles around for a breast when it is hungry, and gradually becomes aware of its mother's wider world. In a continuum family, there is no question of "letting go." The mother's body is warm and her arms comforting, but it's only a matter of months before that wider world becomes too tempting. Continuum babies wriggle out of their mother's arms when they are ready.

The Yequana Indians never worry over the possibility of "giving too much," as Peggy McMahon of *Mothering* and most of the rest of us do, afraid of making our children too dependent. Instinct and the experience of thousands of years have taught the Yequana that "the object of a child's activities *is* the development of self-reliance."

And as Jean Liedloff goes on to explain, "The growth of independence and the power to mature emotionally spring largely from the in-arms relationship in all its aspects. One cannot therefore become independent of the mother, except *through* her, through her playing her correct role, giving the in-arms experience and allowing one to graduate from it upon fulfillment."

When Vita was two and a half, I sat down in the rocking chair all set to nurse her to sleep. She suckled for a couple of seconds and then pulled herself up. "No nuss," she said, looking at me with her big eyes. She never nursed again. When Ishmael was three and a half and Vita just a week old, he said, "I think I can sleep through the night in my own bed now." He has ever since.

Although we had been trying to "cut the apron strings" when we sent Ishmael to camp, by denying him the comfort of our arms, so to speak, we made him more dependent than ever. He didn't leave us again, even for one night, for six years. But then, as if he finally felt fulfilled (the way Vita did when she said, "No nuss"), he decided to spend five weeks in Vermont, playing chamber music at a music festival.

Of the thirty-five or so performing musicians, Ishmael was the youngest by three years. Most of the other participants were in their middle twenties. This was no camp, with counselors to tell you when to go to bed at night. He was responsible for remembering when he had rehearsals scheduled and for getting to them (often two miles away in town); for getting to meals in the cafeteria; for doing his own laundry and dressing decently for concerts; for organizing his own practice times and setting priorities for what music to practice; and for finding time to get a little sleep.

Ishmael has never been known for his practical skills and in any case, at home I had always cooked and cleaned for him. I did his laundry and mailed his letters. He wasn't at all "prepared" for leaving home, and yet he learned fast, out of desire and the necessity his choice had imposed. He had plenty of minor mishaps and a couple of major ones, of course. Certainly he missed us as much as we missed him. And yet he never wavered — the wider world was too tempting. He had been determined to go to this festival. The music and the people kept him there:

Dear Nancy, Bob and Vita,

I got your letters today, which made me very happy, and I thought I would write back immediately, since I'm not sure I'll have much time in the evenings to write before you visit. I've already started trying to solve the crossword puzzles in Vita's *Yearly News Report*. They're hard! I blow the goose whistle often, also. It produces a great variety of pitches. As I was walking to the dormitory today after being dropped off by Peter Stumpf, who drove me back from playing on the concert hall piano, I really surprised myself by starting to sing Schumann's piece, "The Two Grenadiers." For the longest time I couldn't figure out what it was. Usually I sing Kurt Weill or songs in fox-trot rhythm from *Die Dreigroschenoper*. I told Peter Stumpf a lot about Tolly-the-cat. I was pleased that he was *very* interested. I told him about Tolly smelling flowers in the garden! Last night there were a whole lot of different people practicing at once, and, at first, I listened to it as one piece, perhaps by an imitator of Bartok, or something by Ives; then I realized that one of the strands of counterpoint was actually the Mendelssohn violin concerto! I must have been very tired. I'm really enjoying *Jude the Obscure*.

I suddenly realize how far away I am from everyone I love. I look forward to seeing you on Sunday. Love, Ishmael

Although it wasn't easy for us having Ishmael gone for so long, we discovered that as long as he was sure of himself, we *could* let him go. Still, that summer couldn't quite erase all those years of questioning and self-doubt on my part. I keep testing my limits. These past few months, for example, in spurts of an almost perverse nature, I have been trying to convince Ishmael to go to Paris to study with the French composer, Oliver Messiaen, as if I need to hear the sound of my own voice suggest to Ishmael that he travel across the Atlantic Ocean without me.

In *Escape from Childhood* John Holt wrote that most of us view the institution of childhood as a kind of idealized protective garden. "But I believe that most young people," he said, "and at earlier and earlier ages, begin to experience childhood not as a garden but as a prison. What I want to do is put a gate, or gates, into the wall of the garden, so that those who find it no longer protective or helpful, but instead confining and humiliating, can move out of it and for a while try living in a larger space."

John, when he talked about children opening the garden gate, was very specific that the gate be the path out of childhood and the entrance into the adult world. Young people, he said, need "to make contact with the larger society around them, and, even more, to play an active, responsible, useful part in it...."

That is the twist, though. Society pressures me to let Vita and Ishmael go, and yet it seldom allows them a reasonable place *to* go. Friends were horrified, yes, when I zipped nine-year-old Ishmael's jacket or helped him tie his shoes, but they were equally horrified when they discovered that he practiced for long hours every day or spent each afternoon composing music. "You are denying him a childhood," they said. Everywhere we look we find arbitrarily set age limits. Vita can't take a painting class because it's for ages fifteen and up. *She* can't join Ishmael at the music festival until she's "older."

"Childhood goes on for far too long," John wrote, and yet even he recognized that while offering children complete access to our adult world, we have to leave them, always, the right to accept or reject as much of it as they please. "If the larger space proves too much for them," he wrote, "they can always come back into the garden."

When John came to visit and watched Bob coddle eight-year-old Vita into getting dressed in the morning — standing her up on her bed, collecting her clothes, and singing to her — he joined in the fun. "This is the way we pull on our socks, pull on our socks, pull on our socks," John sang, "This is the way we pull on our socks so early in the morning!"

In speaking of children in the walled garden he had written, "I do not want to destroy their garden or kick them out of it. If they like it, by all means let them stay in it."

He knew that Vita still needed her garden, for whatever reason, and that it would take her years of gradual experimentation before she would decide to step out of the garden for good. For Ishmael, the music festival was a first step outside the garden and yet for him, now, a trip across the ocean just wouldn't allow him easy enough access back in.

As for me, still feeling those old pressures, I keep testing the gates to make sure that they'll swing open when Ishmael wants them to. That, of course, is ridiculous, as Ishmael well knows. In continuum families babies wriggle out of their mother's arms. For a mother simply to put her child down (test the gates) would constitute neglect. It's as if in this society we've gotten everything backwards. We feel that we are actually harming our children, "disempowering" them, if we *don't* put them down.

John saw life as "a curve of continual growth and change" and he couldn't help but lament the modern-day notion that at some specific point (usually upon leaving school) the child should suddenly be expected to walk (or be shoved) out of the garden, get a job, and metamorphose into an adult. He called this modern-day rite of passage "The Great Divide" — the break in the curve.

Of course, when people told me to send Ishmael to kindergarten because he needed to spend time away from us, what they were thinking, I'm sure, was that it was best to begin, even then, to prepare him for adulthood and that by starting so early he would never have to experience that abrupt "break."

In theory, the idea of the gradual curve is not new or even radical. For most people, in fact, the gradual curve is what school is all about. They see it as the perfect way for children to take their first tentative steps out into the real world, imagining, almost paradoxically, that school can actually protect children from the real world at the same time.

As Peter Marin and Allen Y. Cohen wrote in *Understanding Drug Use*, "We think of schools as the 'real world': a fixed pattern into which we set the young like furniture. We want so badly to protect and steer them; we want to civilize them, train them, warn them, ready them.

In our zeal to keep them safe we maintain a snug void called schooling and the no-man's-waster of adolescence; we trap them there and try to impose upon them the myth of a nonexistent world."

And, just like Glenda Bissex's point about reading and writing being "meaningless and disembodied if they are regarded as ends in themselves," Marin and Cohen go on to say that in school "we talk to children incessantly about balance and adjustment — but balance *between* what, adjustment *to* what?"

We can never honestly protect children by keeping them away from what is real. Nor can we ever hope to prepare them for reality that way. When John Holt used to say, "Never think in terms of practicing music," he meant, "Don't unpack your instrument with the intention of *preparing* to play real music someday. Play real music *now*. Whether you are playing Kreutzer etudes or even just open strings for sound, make music. And if you feel that you can't make music like that, don't bother — go on to Mozart sonatas and Bach suites and play what notes you can." The only way we can ever prepare ourselves to play music is by actually playing it. Likewise, the only way to prepare for the real world is to live in it.

In *The Continuum Concept* Jean Liedloff tells the story of a two-year-old girl attempting to grate manioc with the women and older girls. At first the little girl picked up a large chunk of manioc and tried to rub it against another girl's grater but the chunk was too large and she kept dropping it. "An affectionate smile and a smaller piece of manioc came from her neighbor, and her mother, ready for the inevitable impulse to show itself, handed her a tiny grating board of her own. The little girl had seen the women grating as long as she could remember and immediately rubbed the nubbin up and down her board like the others." At two, this child was already able to take a step out of the garden and was given a warm welcome into the adult world. How different from childhood in our culture.

Perhaps one reason that, for the Yequana Indians, the transition between childhood and adulthood is so smooth is that their perception of life in the adult world is so unlike ours. When friends told me that Ishmael needed to be with real people (i.e. not just Bob and me) out in the real world (school) they were hinting that a little pain and unhappiness might do him good.

"Ishmael is going to have to learn to leave his garden filled with love, care, and respect," they were saying, "and gradually learn to cope in an environment filled with arbitrariness, competitiveness and even, occasionally, viciousness."

Little Yequana children wriggle eagerly out of their mother's arms to join the adult world, but what children would do that, anywhere, if they didn't perceive the adult world to hold within it, like their child's garden, those very same qualities of love, care, and respect? No wonder "letting go" is such an issue for us. If we honestly believe that the world is a terrible place, then it really is hard to imagine children ever moving out into it without a push. Yet what truly caring parent would ever knowingly push a child into such a place?

In any case, even if it *were* desirable to "ease" children into the adult world, school (the institutional response to the way our society as a whole views childhood) could never adequately do the job, as long as it persists in functioning as a purgatory between childhood and adulthood. Christopher Robin, Pooh's friend and the son of A.A. Milne, complained in his autobiography that because his father was a writer, he couldn't simply go into his father's business when he graduated from Cambridge. Suddenly, he found himself out in the real world and on his own for the first time, groping around blindly for something to do. Oh Christopher Robin, I laughed when I read that passage, did you really think that you were the only one who has ever been in that predicament?

Even if some of us *do* leave school knowing what we want to do, though — even if we don't feel totally stranded on the far side of the garden wall — the truth is that for all of us, our transition into the adult world was warped, delayed, and interfered with by our school experience. It is as if school actually prevented us from taking experimental steps out of the garden, by never allowing us to discover what we really cared about. How different it would have been if our teachers said, "Pursue what you love and what interests you. We are here, not to interfere, but to help in any way we can."

As much as possible, considering our inevitable blinders, Bob and I tried to give Vita and Ishmael just that kind of freedom and support. Almost never did we say, "Vita, it's time to put away the paste and paper and do spelling," but only, "Do you have enough paste?" Because we never taught the kids to think that "School is where we learn things; home is where we take a vacation from school and learning," they have always considered their work to be integrated with the rest of their lives.

When they wake up in the morning they look at the work — not the school work — that they want to do for the day and they figure out how to organize it within the limits of time and family obligations.

"Do you think I'll have time to work through all my pieces and then try them from memory?" Ishmael wonders. "Or maybe I should just concentrate on the technical problems today and work on memory tomorrow. The thing is, I'd like to have time to start copying the wind piece."

Vita wonders if Benji is going to want the Christmas cards she makes for him in October as he did last year. "I still have some Santas to cut out," she says, "and that's going to take hours. But probably I should be making the invitations to my recital first."

Schoolwork is just another aspect of their work as a whole. "As soon as I finish writing the second act of the libretto I'd like to get back to doing math," Ishmael tells me.

And Vita, trying to organize Bob to help her with German, says, "Daddy, I don't think we are at all prepared for Frau Mapes this week. We really need to spend time practicing subjunctives."

For most children, the very act of going to school and coming home again (even changing from school clothes to play clothes) splits up their lives. School is where they work — and yet the work is *given to them*, as if on loan, and judged by people other than themselves. It is not theirs to explore and experiment with. They aren't even allowed real tools to work with, the way the little Yequana girl was when her mother gave her the miniature grating board and the piece of manioc. At home, children *do* have some control over their work, but continually we diminish it in their eyes by referring to it as "play." The most we allow older children are hobbies.

"What are your hobbies?" a TV interviewer once asked Ishmael. Totally unprepared for the question, Ishmael put his hand up to his forehead, as if it was going to require some deep thought. For a minute I wondered if he even knew what a hobby was.

"Um, uh, um, well, I guess there's philosophy," he finally said lamely, hoping, I suppose, that it might count as a hobby since it isn't listed as a required course on the New York State high school curriculum.

"Philosophy?" the reporter asked incredulously. "Come on now." And then, implying that philosophy was too serious and important a subject to be a mere hobby, he asked, "Don't you have any *real* hobbies, like collecting stamps or anything?"

"No," Ishmael said, resigning himself to looking like a thorough misfit.

When Vita was in the hospital, though, and the doctor asked her what her hobbies were as he poked and thumped her, she was prepared. "I like art," she said, "and I play the violin and the piano."

"You do a lot," said the doctor, well satisfied that at least mentally, Vita was normal.

She was pleased to be off the hook and yet I could see that she was disturbed. Was she lying? she wondered. Or could it really be that her art and music were simply pastimes, fun things to fool around with now but not anything to consider pursuing when she grew up?

Fortunately, her disturbance quickly passed, and yet for me, it couldn't help but linger. How lucky she is, I thought almost angrily. After all, unlike Vita and Ishmael, whose work *is* the connecting link between their childhood and their adulthood, most children are trained to believe that they can never do real work of their own or hope to take charge of it until they leave school. As long as school and society perpetuate the myth that the split in children's lives between work and play is normal, children *will* be "disempowered," no matter how hard we try to let go. Vita and Ishmael, meanwhile, simply because of the way they view their work, can metamorphose into adults (and are doing so) in much the way, as Jean Liedloff says, children have since time began. Whether I "give too much" seems to be irrelevant.

Although Vita and Ishmael are realists and know something of both history and current events, not to mention the inside of ambulances and hospitals, they refuse to believe that the adult world is necessarily cold and cruel. Instead, they see it as a larger and more interesting extension of the world they already know. They are convinced that in a pinch it will always be possible to carry along a little extra bundle of love and care to pull them through, the way Vita did when she was sick. Just as they have pursued their work within the garden of childhood, so they are convinced that when they are ready, they will find ways to focus their interests — test and experiment with them — within the larger and more complex space of adulthood.

"Besides piano, composition is the other great project of my life," Ishmael wrote recently to Lillian Kallir and Claude Frank, professors of piano at The Mannes College of Music. "Hitherto I have been able to put large amounts of time into both, largely on account of my being educated at home since the second grade. Now I find myself having to look forward to the problem of how to achieve a similar disposal of time at an institution like Mannes." Growing up, for Ishmael, simply means finding ways to continue his work.

Ishmael probably knew from the day he first touched a piano that he could never live without one. Yet that has never meant that, thanks to some lucky twist of fate, his transition into adulthood will automatically be simpler and easier than it was for the rest of us. He has always known that it is not enough to ask the question, "Do I want to be a musician?" and to answer "Yes."

He knows that to be a musician is only a starting point — a "beginning," to use the words of one of his favorite poets, T.S. Eliot: "What we call the beginning is often the end/And to make an end is to make a beginning./The end is where we start from..."

Although Ishmael has certainly set out on his journey, he hasn't yet shut the garden gate behind him. One of the big questions he is still grappling with is, "How do I learn to work as a musician?"

When he was twelve, he gave his first full-length recital. He worked so hard to prepare for it that it was inconceivable to him, then, that he could ever play more than one recital a year. This year, though, he gave two recitals and several chamber music performances and played in a piano competition (which he won). Over time he has come to be a better judge of how long it will take him to memorize a piece, so that he doesn't end up allowing too much time, or too little. He is learning what it feels like to be confident that a piece is "ready." He is learning how to prepare, both mentally and physically, on the day of a performance — learning what and when to eat, what to practice, how much exercise to get and how much warm-up time to allow. Most exciting, he is discovering how pieces change for him from performance to performance and to look forward to that change rather than just fearing it.

But he is learning more than just how to understand and be more aware of his internal responses to music. He, and Vita, too, are learning how to work within the realm of the marketplace — almost, it sometimes seems, as if they are simply exploring another side to their work. This has been the real surprise for me, since until they taught me otherwise, I was convinced that at least in childhood there had to be a separation between people's paid work and their interests. That is, I figured that when you were a kid, money had to be an end in itself — that the most you could expect was to mow lawns or to babysit. I never imagined that it might be possible for a child to get a paying job dancing, or painting, or studying insects, or, God forbid, playing the piano.

Still, I was convinced that children should work and earn money (in preparation for adulthood, naturally!). When Vita and Ishmael came along, though, everything changed. I mean, what was I supposed to do, interrupt Ishmael, hard at work on his cello sonata, and suggest that he go out and shovel sidewalks? Or tell Vita to put down her violin and see if the neighbors wanted their lawn raked? Yet, as in all things, when they were ready, they simply went out and found paid work, never imagining for a minute that they couldn't earn money doing what they knew best.

Last year they earned over a thousand dollars by playing in concerts and recitals, accompanying other players, and winning prize money in competitions. Vita earned a tidy sum, too, with her Christmas card business. Yet it hasn't always been clear sailing as they go about learning how to expose themselves to the marketplace without compromising their own work, either in terms of quality or time.

All too often, when they've worked as accompanists, Vita and Ishmael have been disappointed by the lack of preparation on the part of the other performer. A job that promised to take just three rehearsals suddenly seems as if it will need ten to get the music into shape. Deciding what to do — how much time and energy to put into it — is always a struggle.

When Ishmael enters a piece in a composition competition he knows that the judges are usually most impressed by long works with massive orchestrations. He has to decide whether to submit what he thinks is his best work or something that might actually please the judges more. Every year Vita agonizes over how to make Christmas cards that are easy to mass produce and yet retain some kind of artistic integrity and interest.

Recently they were both asked to play some four-hand piano music as part of a concert series at a local winery.

"Nothing too dissonant," the organizer warned. But they already had their hearts set on some pieces by Stravinsky. "Let's just say they are by *Ivan* Stravinsky," Ishmael suggested, "You know, Stravinsky's great, great grandfather!"

Although earning money seems to be naturally continuous with doing the work he loves, just how he will choose to do that work is the big question that Ishmael is only beginning to face as he looks around for new teachers and starts to come to some decision about possible study at a music conservatory. To me, he has often seemed to be full of preconceptions. People have been feeding him on stereotypes for years. "The music world is impossible to get into," they say. "A musician's life is hell."

Often, the ways he has posed his choices to himself have seemed too narrow and conventional. "Should I be a composer and try to get a well-paying job at a university?" he asks conservatively. "I don't want my wife to support me like all the other composers I know. Or would it be better to live in New York City, writing grand operas and accompanying dance classes (or driving a taxi) to pay the rent? Should I try to be a concert pianist even if I have to spend my life in hotels, airports, and recording studios? Or should I be content to eke out my living playing occasional concerts in second rate halls, but making great music?"

Slowly, though, and especially as he has begun to have to make choices ("I think I'd rather work with David Borden in his electronic music studio than study Italian this fall"), Ishmael is beginning to see just how many possibilities there really are, and that, whatever direction he eventually decides to take, it doesn't have to be permanently carved in stone. Most important, he is coming to see that whatever he decides, he has to find environments in which he can do his chosen work as productively and with as much creative stimulation as possible.

For Vita, meanwhile, there is an interesting pull, since although she can't imagine ever doing work that she doesn't love, she tends to want to preserve her art and music for a more private sphere. "I never want to be like Susan Andrews who has to stay up all night during the weeks before Christmas making dolls that she doesn't even like," Vita says.

These days if you ask her how she plans to earn her livelihood when she grows up she'll probably say, "I want to work in a sewing store selling material, lace, and ribbons, or do what I do at the food co-op — bag nuts and raisins and cut cheese." Where Vita's path is leading her I'm not sure. *How* it is leading her is continually fascinating.

Sometimes I get impatient with the process. It's so slow and the kids can seem so incredibly naive. ("Vita, what makes you think that if you were an artist you'd have to be like Susan Andrews? Besides, don't you think cutting cheese might ever get boring?") Sometimes, too, they still take me by surprise. For a while I was prepared to say, for example, that teenaged alienation is absolutely unnecessary, at least for kids living outside the purgatory of school and peer pressure. But while alienation is a poor way to describe it, learning to become separate isn't ever easy for kids.

I see Ishmael, determined to develop his own ideas (about religion, philosophy, politics, even people) and to test them independently of us. Sometimes I feel his uncertainty, even fear, as if he is convinced that his independence — his questioning — will wound us in some way. Sometimes we are able to reassure him. Sometimes he doesn't seem to want to be reassured. For all children, I think, there is a time when they are sure that their parents are perfect. Discovering that they aren't is always difficult, as it is now, for Ishmael. And yet I can see his relief, too, as he realizes that like him we are, after all, only human.

As the time draws nearer, I can already feel how painful it will be for me as Vita and Ishmael finally close the garden gate behind them. I know that it is inevitable, though, and even desirable, and that no matter how often I ask them if they've had enough to eat or tell them to be careful crossing the street when they walk into town, I can't hold them back.

"Oh Ishmael," I said the other day, thinking about his plans to go away to study music, "Are you sure you can bear to leave home?"

"I don't know," he said, "but it seems like the only way I'm going to be able to do what I really want to do."

"They belong simultaneously to the family *and* the world," Peter Marin and Allen Cohen wrote of children like Vita and Ishmael. "Their lives will warm and reward them, teach them, test and trouble them. But there is nothing strange or novel about that. The young have always moved outward and into the world to learn what it is really like to be alive."

More and more I find myself feeling the first hints of the pain of loss as Ishmael and Vita move outward. Often people say, "Soon it's going to be time for you to think about YOU, Nancy," implying that although I have been admirably self-sacrificing all these years, that must change if I don't want to be left with a gaping hole in my life when Ishmael and Vita really do leave. Always I find myself wondering how I can ever convince people that I have never been self-sacrificing, that almost certainly *none* of us could have accomplished what we have accomplished if all of us — me included — hadn't been determined to do what we loved most. I wonder how I can ever explain that for everything I have given to Ishmael and Vita, they have repaid me a hundred times over by showing me just how rich and meaningful life can really be.

It was T.S. Eliot, again, who said at the end of his *Four Quartets,* "We shall not cease from exploration/And the end of all our exploring/Will be to arrive where we started/And to know the place for the first time." Vita and Ishmael are truly living out those words, and every day they give them back to me with renewed force and conviction. Watching them wake up each morning, still determined to use everything they see, touch, and hear to feed their creativity, still determined to explore every inch of the territory available to them, has led me back to memories, not just of the giggles and uncontainable joy of the children I watched at the zoo, but back to memories of my own childhood. Watching Vita and Ishmael helped me to realize that my afternoons at the zoo, and, before that, the hours I spent building miniature towns in the granite banks of a dry stream bed, the times I read poetry in the old oak, and the plays, soirees, and musical tea parties I put on in my friend's attic, were not simply ways I chose to escape my homework. They were part of my own serious childhood work. Only as I have watched Vita and Ishmael begin to move outward have I realized that this work was the beginning of a continuous thread that would lead me into adult life and shape my adult work as a writer — work, I see now, that is as worthy of respect and consideration as a child's lingering and skipping. Perhaps the most important thing Ishmael and Vita will have left me with is the realization that the whole notion of escapism is irrelevant to the lives of children. Children discover the real world in every nook and cranny of their lives. And if doing what they love most is all in a day's work for them, it can be for me, too, and for all of us.

Meanwhile, whatever paths my children choose, I know they will be the right ones. Wherever they go, it will be to see the place for the first time, and to show it to me, too, as if it were new — reminding me, always, what it really means to be alive.

About the Author

Nancy Wallace is the author of the book *Better Than School* and numerous articles about homeschooling and how children learn. Her writing has been published in *Mothering, Inquiry, The Boston Globe, Blair and Ketchum's Country Journal,* and other publications, and she is a regular contributor to *Growing Without Schooling* magazine. She has discussed her ideas on several radio and television shows, and has spoken to groups of parents, teachers, and students.

Nancy now lives in Philadelphia, where she manages to combine her work as a mother, teacher, writer, and more and more as a collaborator with her children, as they grow up and begin to take *her* work more seriously. Currently, Nancy is writing fiction, looking at childhood from other angles, and yet always returning to what her children show her about themselves and the way they think.

Holt Associates is a clearinghouse for information about home education, children's learning, and the work of the late author/ educator John Holt. Write for information about our catalogue of books (including Nancy Wallace's first book, *Better Than School*), and about *Growing Without Schooling* magazine:

2269 Massachusetts Avenue,
Cambridge MA 02140